FINDING THE
WILD WEST:
THE MOUNTAIN
WEST

FINDING THE WILD WEST: THE MOUNTAIN WEST

NEVADA, UTAH, COLORADO, WYOMING, AND MONTANA

MIKE COX

TWODOT®

ESSEX, CONNECTICUT
HELENA, MONTANA

A · TWODOT® · BOOK

An imprint and registered trademark of Globe Pequot, the trade division of
The Rowman & Littlefield Publishing Group, Inc.
4501 Forbes Blvd., Ste. 200
Lanham, MD 20706
www.rowman.com

Distributed by NATIONAL BOOK NETWORK

British Library Cataloguing in Publication Information available

Library of Congress Cataloging-in-Publication Data

Names: Cox, Mike, 1948- author.
Title: Finding The Wild West : The Mountain West. Nevada, Utah, Colorado,
    Wyoming, and Montana / Mike Cox.
Description: Essex, Connecticut : TwoDot, [2022] | Series: Finding the wild
    west series | Includes index.
Identifiers: LCCN 2022026756 (print) | LCCN 2022026757 (ebook) | ISBN
    9781493064151 (paperback) | ISBN 9781493064168 (epub)
Subjects: LCSH: West (U.S.)—Description and travel. | Historic sites—West
    (U.S.)—Guidebooks. | West (U.S.)—History. | Historic sites—Rocky
    Mountains Region—Guidebooks. | Rocky Mountains Region—History.
Classification: LCC F592 .C85 2022 (print) | LCC F592 (ebook) | DDC
    917.804—dc23/eng/20220608
LC record available at https://lccn.loc.gov/2022026756
LC ebook record available at https://lccn.loc.gov/2022026757

Writers typically dedicate their books to a particular person, but this book is dedicated to a singularly spiritual moment in the once Wild West and the three people who shared it with me. On June 20, 2016, on our way to the annual Western Writers of America conference, Beverly Waak and I, along with our friends Preston and Harriet Lewis, visited the Little Bighorn Battlefield National Monument. In this historic place where two cultures collided so violently, what we perceived, lingering over the still-remote landscape like traces of gun smoke, was an overwhelming sense of peace. At the circular memorial commissioned by the Lakota to honor their fallen warriors, I happened to look up into a dark blue Montana sky. Having traveled to a lot of places over many decades, I had never seen anything like this: a long, high, thin cloud that looked very much like a giant eagle feather. Beverly, Harriet, and Preston saw it, too. Freak of weather? Somehow, it didn't feel like that. Rather, it was as if the sky, in concert with the wind and the sun, wanted to remind us with its rendering of such a sacred American Indian icon that no matter what, all of us are connected—to each other, to the past, and to the land.

—Mike Cox

CONTENTS

PREFACE: FINDING THE WILD WEST

Ain't nothing better than riding a fine horse in a new country.
—Gus McCrea in *Lonesome Dove*

Like most Baby Boomers, I learned about the Old West in the mid-1950s and early 1960s watching black-and-white television westerns and John Wayne movies in color. But that was Hollywood's Old West.

Thanks largely to my late granddad, L.A. Wilke, I began to learn about the real Old West. He was born in Central Texas in the fading days of that era, just long enough ago to have learned how to ride a horse well before he ever got behind the wheel of an automobile. Too, as a youngster and later as a newspaperman, he met some notable Wild West figures, from Buffalo Bill Cody to old Texas Rangers who had fought Comanches. A fine storyteller, he shared his experiences with me. Also, he passed his copies of *True West* and *Frontier Times* on to me. At the time, his friend Joe Small published both magazines in Austin, where I grew up.

Even before I started reading nonfiction Western magazines and books, again thanks to Granddad, I got to visit some Old West historic sites when they were still just abandoned ruins. With him, as a first grader I prowled around old Fort Davis in West Texas well before the federal government stabilized it as a National Historic Site. Later, Granddad took me to several southwest New Mexico ghost towns, including Shakespeare, Hillsboro, and Kingston. This was in 1964, when many of that state's roadways were not yet paved. In that desert high country, I experienced for the first time the still-vast openness of the West and the sense of adventure in exploring an old place new to me.

So why was the West wild?

I think you will come to understand the "why" when you experience the "where" of the Wild West. Though many of the sites described in these books are in populated areas, some are as remote or more remote than they were back in the Wild West's heyday. In visiting these sites, say a ghost town well off the beaten path, you should be able to feel the reason why the West was wild. When I stand in the middle of nowhere, distant from nothing, I feel the sense of freedom that must have driven so much of human behavior in frontier times. In such emptiness, usually scenic, it's easy to believe you can do anything you, by God, want to, be it bad or good.

Some see the West as being all the states west of the Mississippi, which includes twenty-three states. Others maintain that the West begins at the ninety-eighth meridian. My belief is that the Mississippi River is what separates the East from the West in the US.

Accordingly, moving from east to west, this series of travel guides divides the West into five regions: along the Mississippi (Louisiana, Arkansas, Iowa, Minnesota, and Missouri); the Great Plains (Oklahoma, Kansas, Nebraska, South Dakota, and North Dakota); the Southwest (Arizona, New Mexico, and Texas); the Mountain West (Colorado, Montana, Nevada, Utah, and Wyoming); and the Pacific West (Alaska, California, Idaho, Oregon, and Washington).

Having described what I consider the West, what constitutes "wild?"

Former Wild West History Association president Robert G. (Bob) McCubbin, a history buff who acquired one of the world's most inclusive collections of Western photographs, ephemera, books, and artifacts, a few years back offered his take on the matter.

"The Wild West was a time and place unique in the history of the world," he wrote. "It took place on the plains, prairies, mountains, and deserts of the American West, from the Mississippi River to the

Pacific Ocean. It began about the time of the California gold rush and was at its height in the 1870s through the 1890s, fading away in the decade after the turn of the twentieth century—as the automobile replaced the horse."

He went on to explain that Wild West does not mean wilderness wild. It means lawless wild. While untamed grandeur was certainly a part of the Wild West, it was the untamed men and women who made the West wild.

"Of course," McCubbin continued, "during the Wild West period there were many good and substantial citizens who went about their business in a law abiding and constructive way. Most of those are forgotten. It's the excitement of the Wild West's bad men, desperadoes, outlaws, gunfighters, and lawmen—many of whom were also, at times, cowboys, scouts, and buffalo hunters—and the dance hall girls and 'shady ladies,' who capture our interest and imagination."

While mostly adhering to McCubbin's definition of the Wild West, I could not stick to it entirely. Some things that happened prior to the California gold rush—Spanish and French colonial efforts, the Louisiana Purchase, the Lewis and Clark Expedition, the exploits of mountain men, the development of the great western trails, and the Mexican War of 1846 to 1848—were critical in shaping the later history of the West. That explains why some of the sites associated with these aspects of history needed to be included in this book.

For the most part, 1900 is the cut-off date for events related in this series of books. But the Wild West did not end at 11:59 p.m. on December 31, 1899. Some places, particularly Arizona, Oklahoma, New Mexico, and far west Texas stayed wild until World War I. Sometimes, events that occurred in the nineteenth century continued to have ramifications in the early twentieth century. An example would be the life and times of Pat Garrett, who killed Billy the Kid in 1881. Garrett himself was shot to death in 1909, so his death site is listed.

The Finding the Wild West series is not intended as a guide to every single historic site in a given city, state, or region. Some towns and cities had to be left out. It would take an encyclopedic, multi-volume work to cover *all* the historical places throughout the western states. I have tried to include the major sites with a Wild West connection, along with some places with great stories you've probably never heard.

These books focus primarily on locations where there is still something to see today. Those sites range from period buildings and ruins to battlefields, historical markers, tombstones, and public art. In addition to historic sites, I have included museums and libraries with collections centered on "those thrilling days of yesteryear." Again, I have *not* listed every museum or every attraction.

A note on directions: Since almost everyone has access to GPS applications or devices, locations are limited to specific addresses with "turn here" or "until you come to" used only when necessary, with the exception of block-row-plot numbers of graves (when available). GPS coordinates are given for more difficult to find locations.

The Wild West has long since been tamed, with nationally franchised fast-food places and big-box stores standing where the buffalo roamed and the deer and the antelope played. Considered another way, however, the Wild West hasn't gone anywhere. It still exists in our collective imagination—a mixture of truth and legend set against the backdrop of one of the world's most spectacular landscapes.

Wild Bill Hickok, Jesse James, George Armstrong Custer, Billy the Kid, Wyatt Earp, and others received a lot of press and rose from the dead as Western icons, but there were many more characters—from outlaws to lawmen, drovers to cattle barons, harlots to preachers—whose stories are yet to be brought to life. Indeed, every tombstone, every historical marker, every monument, every ghost town, every historic site, every place name, every structure, every person has a story to tell. Like a modern-day prospector, all you need to do is pack these books in your saddlebag, mount up, and ride out in search of the Wild West.

—Mike Cox
Wimberley, Texas

INTRODUCTION: THE MOUNTAIN WEST

RANGING FROM CANADA TO THE RIO GRANDE, THE ROCKY MOUN-
tains dominate the landscape and the history of the Mountain West.
The Rockies posed a potentially deadly hazard to western emigrants,
but the precious metals created in the ancient geological upheaval
of their rising provided wealth to a growing nation. And the snow-
topped mountains furnished the water, wildlife, and wood needed to
sustain settlement.

The first territory established in the Mountain West was Utah.
Congress took that action in 1850, only three years after Brigham
Young led a party of Mormon pioneers to the Great Salt Lake Valley.
When Young and the vanguard of his followers arrived in 1847, the
future territory was part of Mexico. A year later, however, the US
took control of the area following its victorious war with Mexico.
Utah continued as a sometimes problematic territory for nearly half a
century until it was admitted to the Union in 1896, the last of the six
Mountain West states to get a star on the flag.

Less than a decade after the discovery of gold in California,
large quantities of the highly sought metal were found in the vicinity
of Pike's Peak in 1859. Congress took portions of Utah, Nebraska,
Kansas, and New Mexico Territories to create Colorado Territory in
February 1861, only three months before the beginning of the Civil
War. Soon after, by treaty the Cheyenne and Arapaho people ceded
most of their lands in Colorado to the US. In 1863 the Utes agreed to
allow settlement on their lands, but by 1873 they had been relegated
to a reservation in the western part of the territory. Having yielded

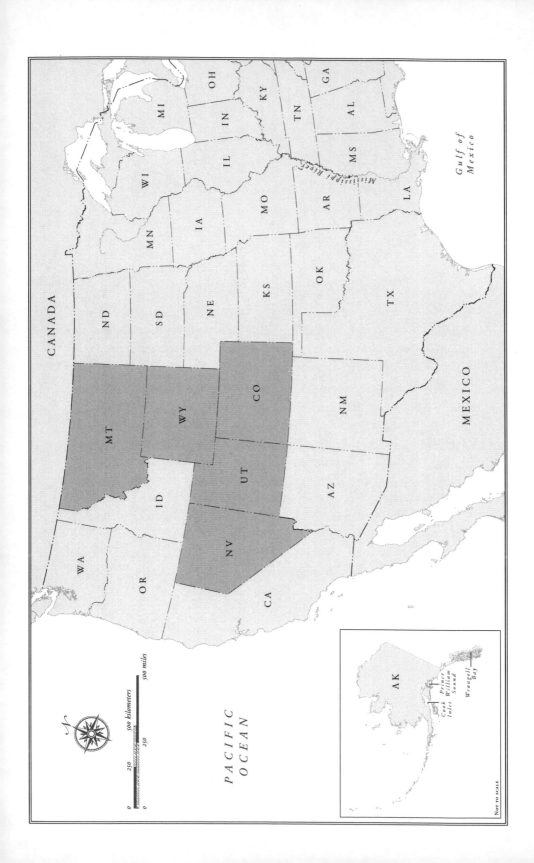

enormous quantities of precious metals, by 1876 the territory had enough residents to become the thirty-eighth state.

Nevada started as a political subdivision of Utah Territory—sprawling Carson County. Following the discovery of the Comstock Lode in 1859, Congress separated Carson County from Utah and designated it Nevada Territory in March 1861. Given the amount of silver and gold coming out of the territory, Congress gave it statehood status in 1864 during the Civil War.

Also in 1864, at the height of the gold mining boom around Virginia City and nearby Nevada City, Congress took more than half of Idaho Territory to form the new territory of Montana. Montana became the forty-first state in 1889.

From portions of Dakota, Idaho, and Utah Territories, Wyoming Territory was established in 1868, with admission to the Union not happening until 1890.

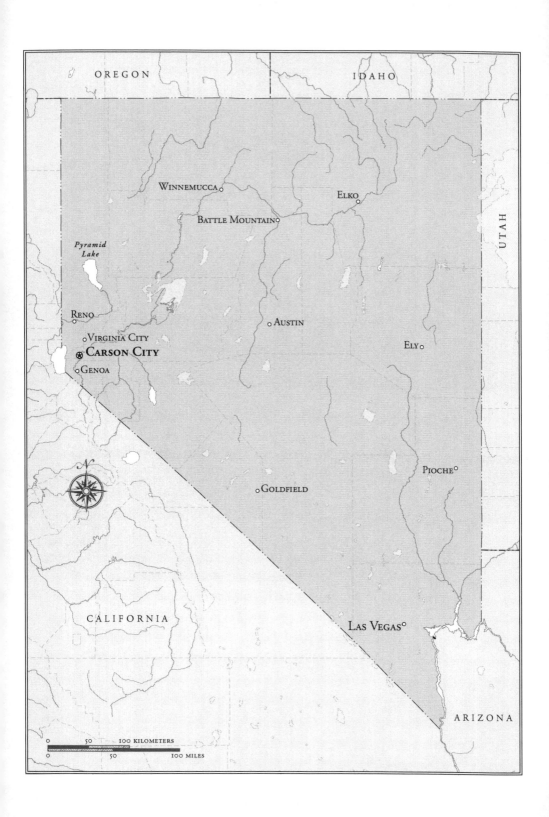

NEVADA

Austin (Larson County)

William Talcott was gathering firewood (others say looking for a lost horse) when he noted a promising ledge of quartz in central Nevada's Pony Canyon, not far from a stagecoach stop called Jacob's Station. He collected samples for analysis and sent the rocks to Virginia City. The assayer's report showed the ore was rich in silver. As word spread, miners descended on the canyon, and their tent city grew into the town of Austin.

By 1865 the community had an estimated ten thousand residents, making it Nevada's second-largest city. At the time, that many residents also made Austin, Nevada, twice as large as Austin, Texas, the Lone Star State's capital. Some have posited that the Nevada city was named after its doppelganger, but most believe the name honored one of its pioneers.

The boomtown got another boost when it gained a railroad connection in 1880. Rail service loses its significance when a carrier has less and less to ship, which is what happened in the 1890s as the ore began to play out at the same time the value of silver declined. A final economic blow came in 1979 when the Nevada legislature voted to make Battle Mountain the county seat.

A $275,000 Sack of Flour

In 1864 Austin merchant Reuel Gridley lost an election bet. Rather than wagering money on the outcome of the city's mayoral race, Gridley declared that if his candidate lost the election, he would tote a fifty-pound bag of flour the length of the town, more than a mile. When his man got beat, Gridley carried out his obligation. Then he put the flour sack up for auction to benefit the US Sanitary Commission, a Red Cross–like organization.

When word spread that the flour sack realized $8,000 in Austin, other communities asked Gridley to put it on the auction block in their town. In a year of traveling all over the West, Gridley raised $275,000 to benefit wounded or sick Civil War soldiers.

Listed on the National Register of Historic Places in 2003, the old **Gridley Store** (247 Water St.) still stands. The Wild West's most famous flour sack survived and is displayed at the Nevada Historical Society Museum in Reno. Reuel Colt Gridley (1829–1870) moved to California in 1866.

BATTLE MOUNTAIN (LARSON COUNTY)

Battle Mountain began as a stop on the transcontinental Central Pacific Railroad in 1869. As for this community's evocative name, historians have not been able to agree on what if any clash of arms Battle Mountain refers to. The most common story is that a prospector named George Tannihill named the surrounding mining district that preceded the founding of the town in commemoration of a fight that he and nearly two dozen other settlers had in 1857 with American Indians in the vicinity. But if it happened, no one has ever uncovered any details.

Whatever led to its naming, the town got another boost in 1880 when the Nevada Central Railroad completed a line connecting Austin to the transcontinental railroad at Battle Mountain. As a supply and shipping point, the town survived the decline of mining in the area that killed or stunted numerous other communities, including Austin.

Battle Mountain has two museums, the **Trail of the 49ers' Interpretive Center** (453 North 2nd St.; 775-635-5720) and the **Battle Mountain Cookhouse Museum** (905 Burns St.; 775-635-8548). The museum focuses on local history, not Western culinary arts, but it is housed in a near-century-old cookhouse moved to town from an area ranch.

BELMONT (NYE COUNTY)

Founded in 1865 as a mining town following the discovery of silver ore in the Toquima Mountains, within two years Belmont had a population of two thousand. The town got another boost in 1867 when the county seat was moved here from Ione. Over the following two decades, area mines produced some $15 million in silver before the ore began to play out. But Belmont never gained a rail connection, and after its primary economic engine careened off the figurative track, the town declined. In 1905 the county seat was relocated to then-booming Tonopah, forty-five miles to the south.

Charlie and Jack Become Unruly

In 1874, two men named Charlie McIntyre and Jack Walker arrived in Belmont and began to explore the town. In the process, perhaps having overindulged in spiritous beverages, they settled a difficulty with a local resident by shooting him. The man survived, but the newcomers were duly arrested.

Not finding that confinement suited their lifestyle, the pair managed to break out of jail and went on the lam. A couple of days later, they were captured and returned to jail. Details are sketchy, but for whatever reason—maybe the shooting victim had died—a delegation of concerned citizens decided there was no need to burden the county's legal system with a trial.

Descending on the sheriff's office and basement lockup, the vigilantes overpowered the sheriff and a deputy, tied them up, and removed McIntyre and Walker from their cells. The high desert town lacking any substantial trees, the citizens group figured out a way to hang the men right there in the jail.

Once they'd asphyxiated, the pair were cut down and taken to the **Belmont Cemetery** on the edge of town (GPS coordinates: N38° 35.06', W116° 52.69') and buried in an unmarked common grave. The double lynching occurred in the old bank building, the ruins of which are still standing, during the construction of the two-story redbrick courthouse that opened in 1876. The ghost town's most impressive surviving structure, it was maintained by the state for a time but was transferred to Nye County in 2012. A nonprofit group now takes care of the property.

CARSON CITY (CONSOLIDATED MUNICIPALITY OF CARSON CITY)

When Frank Hall shot an eagle, then had it mounted and hung over the door of the trading post that he and five others opened in 1851 on the Emigrant Trail, it seemed logical to call the place Eagle Station. The store went through several owners before Abraham Curry and other investors bought it and the entire surrounding valley in 1858. They had a townsite surveyed and named it Carson City for scout Kit Carson. In 1861, when Congress cut Utah Territory in half to create Nevada Territory, Carson City became the capital. With statehood coming three years later, it remained the seat of government.

With many of its nineteenth-century buildings still standing, Carson City is considered one of the best unreconstructed early-day mining towns in Nevada. Among the vintage structures are the 1871 Greek Revival **Lander County Courthouse** (122 Main St.), the 1866 **City Hall** (90 South St.), and the **St. Charles Hotel** (310 South Carson St.; 775-882-1887). Built in 1862, the St. Charles is the oldest continuously operating hotel in Nevada. These buildings are among forty-four National Register of Historic Places or properties in Carson City.

Built in 1863 by Lemuel "Sandy" Bowers and his wife Alison "Eilley" Orrum Bowers, the sixteen-room **Bowers Mansion** is a monument to nineteenth-century nouveau riche extravagance. Having made separate fortunes in silver mining, the couple spent $400,000 building an elegant stone mansion inspired by Mrs. Bowers's memory of fine homes in her native Scotland. The couple traveled to Europe, spending additional hundreds of thousands of dollars collecting furniture and fine art to go inside their new home.

Eilley made her share of their wealth by seeing the future—or at least pretending to. Running a boardinghouse in Gold Hill, Nevada, before she married Bowers, she supplemented her income as a crystal ball–gazing fortune-teller. If her clients didn't have cash, Eilley cheerfully accepted mining claims. Soon she became Nevada's first millionaire.

Poor money management and the decline of silver mining cost the couple their fortune. When her husband died in 1874, Eilley converted their mansion into a boardinghouse and special-event venue. But two years later, she sold her property and spent the rest of her life predicting good fortune for others.

Bowers Mansion Regional Park (4005 Bowers Mansion Rd.; 775-849-1825) is located ten miles north of Carson City off US 395. The mansion saw a succession of private owners before Washoe County purchased it in 1946. Restored and filled with period furniture, the old house is the centerpiece of a public park operated by the county.

Prize Fighting Enters the Ring

Shortly after the Nevada legislature legalized prize fighting, promoter Dan Stuart staged a world championship bout between reigning heavyweight titlist "Gentleman Jim" Corbett and Robert Fitzsimmons in Carson City. Fitzsimmons won the fourteen-round fight, which took place March 17, 1897, and was seen by thousands. It also was the first successfully filmed sporting event, and some of the original footage is preserved in the Library of Congress. A historical marker at East Musser and North Harbin Streets, Carson City, stands at the site of the arena.

In 1869 the federal government opened a mint in Carson City to produce coins from Nevada's silver mines. The first coins were shipped in 1870. Excepting a four-year period from 1885 to 1889, the mint stamped coins until 1893. After that, the two-story stone **Old US Mint** building (with basement) was used as a federal assay office until 1933. Six years later the government sold the building to the state, and it became a museum. The **Nevada State Museum** (600 North Carson St.; 775-687-4810) showcases the state's history from the days of the dinosaur forward. The old mint's original coin press remains in the building and is still workable, used occasionally to produce commemorative coins.

The nation's first transcontinental railroad cut across the top of Nevada, and several score other railroads operating in the state over the years carried precious metal, people, and goods. Other than the Central Pacific, the state's most storied rail line was the Virginia and Truckee, begun in 1869. During its peak years it ran from Reno to Carson City, splitting from there to connect with Virginia City and Minden.

The **Nevada State Railroad Museum** (2180 South Carson St.; 775-687-6953) has a substantial collection of vintage rolling stock, including an 1875 wood-burning steam locomotive and other cars used by the V&T. Back in operation as a heritage railroad, the V&T runs a restored vintage train between Carson City and Virginia City. Schedule and tickets are available online at https://vtrailway.com or at the **V&T Depot** (4650 Eastgate Siding Rd.; 775-291-0208).

Built in 1871 of stone quarried by convicts, the **Nevada State Capitol** (101 North Carson St.) is both architecturally and historically interesting. A two-story structure with a basement and a center cupola, the building was expanded in 1905 and again in 1914. Exhibits in the building relate the history of the capitol and the state.

Devastating fires leveled many an early-day western town, making a volunteer fire department vital to any community. Organized in 1863, the Warren Engine Company No. 1 is the oldest volunteer fire department west of the Mississippi. Its volunteer firefighters work with the Carson City Fire Department in handling calls. Located in the city's central fire station, the **Carson City Fire Museum** (777 South Stewart St.; 775-887-2210) features antique firefighting gear, wagons, and trucks.

ELKO (ELKO COUNTY)

Elko is one of five towns developed as the Central Pacific Railroad pushed through Nevada in 1868 to connect with the west-bound Union Pacific in Utah. One version of how it got its name has a railroad official simply adding an "o" to elk, a plentiful game animal in the Mountain West. Another theory is that it came from "elko," a Shoshone word for "rocks piled on one another." With its transcontinental rail connection, Elko became a commercial center for ranchers and mining interests. The largest community for 130 miles around, the city's motto is "The Heart of Northeast Nevada."

The twenty-thousand-square-foot **Northeastern Nevada Museum** (1515 Idaho St.; 775-738-3418) has six galleries focused on northeastern Nevada history, wildlife, and art.

The California Trail

The California Trail passed near present Elko, and its well-worn ruts are still visible at some points. Jointly operated by the federal Bureau of Land Management and the Southern Nevada Conservancy, the **California Trail Interpretive Center**'s (1 Interpretive Center Way, I-80 at Hunter exit 292; 775-738-1849) exhibits tell the story of the two-thousand-mile route that from 1841 to 1869 brought an estimated quarter-million people to California—many of them in search of gold. Fifty miles northeast of Elko, still in Elko County, the **Trail of the 49ers' Interpretive Center** (436 6th St.; 775-752-3540) also is devoted to this important Western route.

ELY (WHITE PINE COUNTY)

A stagecoach stop in eastern Nevada near the Schell Creek Range, known as the Murray Creek Station, developed into a small community following the 1870 discovery of gold and silver in the area. The ore was not high quality, but the copper in the area was plentiful and that later brought on a boom.

The town that grew near the stagecoach station was named in 1878 for Smith Ely, president of Selby Copper Mining and Smelting. Copper mining continued as the town's economic mainstay for decades. The history of the town and county is the focus of the **White Pine Public Museum** (2000 Aultman St.; 775-289-4710). Exhibits range from American Indian artifacts and other cultural items to surveyor's instruments to mining equipment and more.

Ward Charcoal Ovens

Resembling giant beehives, a row of six thirty-foot-tall, twenty-seven-foot-diameter stone charcoal ovens dating to the 1870s are the centerpiece of the **Ward Charcoal Ovens State Historic Park** (775-289-1693). They were used to convert piñon and pine into the charcoal needed to fire the ore smelters in nearby Ward, long since a ghost town. After the mines shut down in 1879, travelers sometimes used the vacant ovens as a safe place to spend the night. They remained privately owned until the state began conservatorship in 1956. Acquiring property around the ovens, the Nevada State Park Commission designated the site a state monument in 1969. The ovens were listed on the National Register of Historic Places in 1971. In 1994, the state opened a seven-hundred-acre state park around the ovens.

The state park is twenty miles south of Ely. Take US 50 south for thirteen miles before turning right at the marked Ward Charcoal Ovens State Park turnoff. Continue for five miles to Cave Valley Road, turn left, and follow it to the site.

One of the best-preserved old-time rail facilities in the nation, the **Nevada Northern Railroad Museum** complex (1100 Avenue A; 775-289-2085) covers the short line's fifty-six-acre train yard. Roughly seventy buildings—from roundhouse to depot—and seventy pieces of rolling stock can be toured or ridden. The railroad was founded in the early 1900s to connect Eureka with the Western Pacific and Southern Pacific Railroads. The copper mines in the area shipped multiple tons of ore over the Nevada Northern, but when the last two mines closed in the 1970s, so did the railroad. In the 1980s, a nonprofit took over the property and began developing the site as a museum. The facility became a National Historic Landmark in 2006. A separate museum on the property, the **East Ely Depot Museum** (775-289-1663) is operated by the state.

EUREKA (EUREKA COUNTY)

Five prospectors found silver ore in the vicinity of what would become Eureka in 1864, but mining did not begin for another five years. The boom came in 1869 when the company that had purchased the prospectors' claim built a smelter that could handle the high lead content ore. As mining in the area expanded, more smokestacks rose. By 1876, Eureka had nineteen smelting plants, and some started referring to it as the "Pittsburgh of the West." A rail connection to the Central Pacific Railroad at Palisade spurred further growth, and by 1878 the town had nine thousand residents. Mining declined in the 1880s and the town began to atrophy.

Fires ravaged Eureka several times in the 1870s, so more brick buildings began going up. One was the **Eureka Opera House** (31 South Main St.; 775-237-6006), built in 1880. Restored in 1993 to serve as a convention center, the two-story building has stone walls two feet thick with a brick façade, iron shutters for the windows, and a slate roof.

Built of locally made red brick and sandstone quarried in the vicinity, the **Eureka County Courthouse** opened in 1880. County residents considered the two-story Victorian structure essentially fireproof. Renovated in 1995, the courthouse (10 South Main St.; 775-237-5530) still serves its original purpose.

Covering both floors of the two-story brick building constructed in 1879 as the office of the *Eureka Sentinel*, the **Eureka Sentinel Museum** (10 North Monroe St.; 775-237-5010) displays the newspaper's original press and related hot-metal printing equipment, as well as exhibits dealing with Eureka County history. The newspaper used the building until 1960.

The Carbonari Massacre

It took sixteen thousand bushels of charcoal a day to keep each of Eureka's nearly two dozen smelters working. Hundreds of men worked at producing and selling the fuel needed to do that. Many were Italians who called themselves *carbonari*, Italian for "charcoal makers." Intending to realize the highest-possible profit margin, the smelter operators lowered the Italians' wages to a predetermined amount across the board. The workers organized and boycotted the smelters, which led to the owners asking the governor to send militia, but he refused. The sheriff, however, led a posse to a carbonari camp south of town and attacked on August 18, 1879, leaving five dead. The killings went unprosecuted, but the workers and owners came to an agreement ending the work stoppage.

In 1983 the Eureka Historical Society placed a marker bearing the names of the slain carbonari in the old **Eureka Cemetery** (Caribou Way and Holly Road; GPS coordinates: N39° 30.61', W115° 58.24').

GENOA (DOUGLAS COUNTY)

Its history tracing to a Mormon trading post opened in 1850, Genoa is Nevada's oldest continuously settled town. Mormon elder Orson Hyde named the town for the Italian city of Genoa, but Nevadans pronounce it differently (juh-NO-ah). Genoa was in Utah Territory originally, but stimulated in part by public meetings held in Genoa, Congress created Nevada Territory in 1861. The town was a Pony Express and stagecoach stop, but by the mid-1860s Virginia City and Reno had surpassed Genoa in size and significance.

"Snowshoe" Thompson

Norwegian-born Jon Torsteinson Rui (who adopted "Thompson" hoping to avoid prejudice) not only faithfully carried the mail to and from Genoa for twenty years—even in the dead of winter when travel was considered all but impossible in the Sierra Nevada—he profoundly influenced a mainstay of modern American recreation. When he started his Genoa-to-Placerville, California, route in 1856, the heavy, ten-foot-long oak slats he attached to his boots to more easily traverse packed snow were known as "snowshoes," which is how he got his nickname. Today, the equipment he had learned to use in his native Norway and later introduced to the culture of the Mountain West are called skis.

Thompson (1827–1876) is buried in **Genoa Cemetery** (off Main Street, between Centennial Drive and Trail Court; 775-720-1627; GPS coordinates: N39° 00.70', W119° 50.59'). A marble stone placed there in 1885 features an engraving of a crossed pair of skis. A historical marker telling of his remarkable feats stands at Jacks Valley Road and Genoa Lane. Nearby, a bronze statue honors him at **Mormon Station State Historic Park** (2295 Main St.; 775-782-2590).

In 1853, Al Livingston built a brick building and opened Livingston's Exchange, the "exchange" involving money for liquor. Frank Fettic bought the saloon in 1884 and renamed it Fettic's Exchange. The business model remained the same, but Fettic catered to gentlemen, allowing no overindulgence, fighting, or any of the other things that were standard in most Wild West watering holes. With a succession of owners since then, the establishment (2282 Main St.; 775-782-3870) is Nevada's oldest continually operating bar. Scenes for numerous movies have been filmed here, including John Wayne's last Western, *The Shootist*.

Rufus Adams and Lawrence Gilman built the Douglas County Courthouse in 1865. A fire that destroyed much of the town in 1910 claimed the original building, but the county restored it to its original appearance. When the county seat was moved to Minden in 1916, the Douglas County School District bought the building for $15 and used it as an elementary school until 1956. The building (2304 Main St.; 775-782-4325) opened as the **Genoa Courthouse Museum** in 1971 and underwent extensive renovation during the American Bicentennial.

Sam Brown's Unhappy Birthday

Sam Brown picked up his bad habit of killing men who didn't need killing in Texas and continued his homicidal ways in California and then Nevada. With little law enforcement in those places during the 1850s, Brown escaped any consequences—legal or otherwise—until he hit Genoa. On July 6, 1861, Brown showed up at a buddy's trial, intent on intimidating the jury. But when the ruffian tried to enter the courtroom, an attorney disarmed him. Later, having gotten his gun back, Brown took a shot at an innkeeper named Henry Van Sickle. He missed, but Van Sickle got his scattergun and galloped off after his assailant. When Van Sickle found Brown, his first shot knocked off Brown's hat and blistered his face. "I've got you," Van Sickle reportedly declared as his finger pulled the double-barrel's other trigger. "And I kills you." Which he did. Three days later a coroner's jury found Van Sickle had not only acted in self-defense, but in killing Brown he had rendered the community a considerable service.

Van Sickle (1822–1894) is buried in **Genoa Cemetery.** A historical marker on State Highway 206 in Genoa (GPS coordinates: N38° 58.37', W119° 50.29') tells of Brown's demise.

The local newspaper that covered the Sam Brown matter was the *Territorial Enterprise*, Nevada's first newspaper. Founded on December 8, 1858, its most famous reporter was Samuel Clemens, later much better known as Mark Twain. The *Enterprise* moved to Carson City in 1859 and a year later to then-booming Virginia City. A historical plaque at the intersection of Genoa Lane and Jackson Valley Road marks the newspaper site.

GOLDFIELD (ESMERALDA COUNTY)

Tom Fisherman, a Shoshone, found gold in the vicinity of Columbia Mountain in 1902. He returned with two miners, and a modest mining camp soon developed. A year later miners discovered more substantial deposits, and the boom was on. Production peaked in 1907, but in less than a decade all that glittered was not Goldfield. A flash flood and three devastating fires hastened its decline. Modern Goldfield is a semi–ghost town.

Virgil Earp, Wyatt Earp's older brother, moved to Goldfield with wife Allie in 1904 hoping to capitalize on the boom. They lived in a boardinghouse, and he worked as a dealer and private policeman for the National Club Saloon. In January 1905 the county sheriff commissioned him as a deputy, but that was only to give him more authority in his security job. A month later he contracted pneumonia and died in Goldfield's hospital, on October 19, 1905.

Despite the various disasters the town has experienced, about a hundred of its old structures remain. The Goldfield Historical Society makes available a walking tour of historic sites and maintains a museum in the restored 1906 **Goldfield Firehouse** (233 Crook Ave.; 775-485-3560). Goldfield's oldest building is the 1905 **Santa Fe Saloon.** Built in 1907, the two-story **Esmeralda County Courthouse** (403 Crook St.) continues in use. The largest structure in town is the 1908 **Goldfield Hotel,** a four-story brick building at US 95 and Columbia Avenue. Transitioning from opulent accommodation to just a place to stay, the hotel closed in 1940, and despite efforts to restore and reopen it, the old hostelry remains vacant, a popular haunt of ghost hunters and vandals.

LAS VEGAS (CLARK COUNTY)

What happens in Las Vegas may stay in Las Vegas, but in Old West days, not much happened. In fact, the city did not even exist in the nineteenth century. It was founded in 1905 by the San Pedro, Los Angeles, and Salt Lake Railroad, but even with the state's legalization of gambling in 1931, it remained a small town until after World War

II. Despite the sprawling neon city's modern-day focus on the next bet, it has one nineteenth-century historic site and two museums of interest to Western history enthusiasts.

The first Euro-American settlement in the Las Vegas Valley was an adobe fort constructed by Mormon pioneers near a spring creek in 1855. One hundred and fifty feet square with fourteen-foot walls, the outpost was a welcome supply point and watering hole for California-bound travelers. The Mormons abandoned the place when US troops moved into Utah a few years later, the beginning of the so-called Utah War. A small detachment of federal troops occupied the fort, renamed Fort Baker, during the Civil War. In 1865 settler Octavius Gass used the fort as his ranch headquarters, calling his holding Los Vegas Rancho. Gass lost the property in 1881, and it went through several owners after that, the old fort surviving several brushes with possible demolition.

The historic downtown property was acquired in 1955 by the Las Vegas Elks Club and conveyed to the City of Las Vegas in 1989. Two years later it became the **Old Mormon Fort State Park** (500 East Washington Ave.; 702-486-3511). The old fort was restored and filled with artifacts and interpretive exhibits. A visitor center was added in 2005.

Las Vegas's first overnight accommodation, Hotel Nevada, opened on January 13, 1906. Later renamed the **Golden Gate Hotel and Casino** (1 Fremont St.; 702-382-6300), it had the city's first casino (operated until 1910 when gambling became illegal), first telephone (the number was 1), and the first of the large electric signs that would become a Las Vegas fixture (though initially it was not a neon sign). The hotel is still open and in its original building, although it has been modernized.

Opened in 1982 at a different location, the **Nevada State Museum-Las Vegas** (309 South Valley View Blvd.; 702-486-5205) moved to a larger, seventy-thousand-square-foot building in 2011. It has a thirteen-thousand-square-foot permanent gallery covering the state's history from the Paleo era to Las Vegas's development as a worldwide tourist destination. The museum also has a larger collection of archival material and ongoing special exhibits.

The museum is on the campus of **Springs Preserve,** a 180-acre complex of restored or reconstructed historic buildings, historical exhibits, botanical gardens, and natural habitat at the springs that first drew settlers to the area. **Clark County Museum** (1830 South Boulder Highway, Henderson; 702-455-7955) is sixteen miles southeast of Las Vegas.

PIOCHE (LINCOLN COUNTY)

Pioche has a hard-to-pronounce name (Pee-oach), but in the early 1870s, it was easy to die in this high-country mining town. Claims that seventy-two people met a violent demise here before someone finally got around to dying naturally are exaggerated (another account says only six people died the hard way before someone got sick and died), but it is believed that more than two score killings took place in Lincoln County from 1870 to 1875. If the numbers are accurate, more people were killed in Pioche than in any five-year period in Tombstone and Dodge City combined.

The town was named for Francois L.A. Pioche, a San Francisco financier who purchased mineral claims and started the Meadow Valley Mining Company in 1869. Fire killed thirteen people and destroyed much of Pioche in 1871, but it rebuilt quickly. At its peak in 1872, it had an estimated population of six thousand. The stagecoach from Palisade, California, which had a rail connection, brought people of all stripes. Pioche also had well-traveled stagecoach connections to Salt Lake City and the mining town of Bullionville. The town supported seventy-two saloons, three "hurdy-gurdy" houses, thirty-two bawdy houses, two daily newspapers, two telegraph offices, two theaters, two breweries, two gravity-fed water systems with street mains and fire plugs, two fire companies, and a livery stable.

Thanks to its flourishing mines, when Pioche became the seat of Lincoln County in 1872, a lot of money flowed through town. But not much of it was going to the county in the form of taxes. Still, the county needed a courthouse. Designed by Edward Danahue and bid out at $16,000, cost overruns quickly mounted as construction on the two-story brick and stone courthouse got under way. County officials issued $75,000 in bonds and even printed local scrip to fund the project and meet the county's other expenses.

When mining activity declined, property values went off the cliff. That, in turn, seriously impacted tax revenue and the county couldn't make interest payments on its obligations, much less on the principal. The Nevada legislature offered some relief in 1907 by approving a plan to redeem the outstanding bonds at 65 percent of face value. Lawmakers also transferred part of the debt to newly created Clark County, which had been part of Lincoln County. Even so, not until 1938 was the debt finally retired. At some point, someone calculated that given inflation, the old county courthouse had cost nearly a million dollars.

The courthouse building (69 Lacour St.; 775-962-5207) stood in disrepair for nearly forty years before it was restored in the 1970s. In 1978 it was listed on the National Register of Historic Places.

By the time Nevada's local and state governments got around to keeping relatively accurate birth and death records, Pioche had long since become a ghost town. Despite the lack of exact numbers, the consensus seems to be that Pioche's **Boot Hill Cemetery** has a hundred or so marked and unmarked graves of those who died violently. Other than being in a remote location with numerous drinking establishments, one common cause of homicide was mining claim encroachments. Rather than argue over real estate matters in court, property owners, or claimants, imported hired guns to perform six-shooter surveys. The Find a Grave database lists sixty-seven burials, all but three occurring between 1870 and 1878. Scratched on the wooden marker of Morgan Courtney is this epitaph: "Feared by some, respected by few, detested by others. Shot in back five times from ambush." His killer was tried and acquitted.

Driving through Pioche on State Highway 322, turn east on Comstock Road. The cemetery is on the left, just south of the Pioche Public Cemetery (GPS coordinates: N37° 56.06', W114° 26.82').

Because of its remote location, when mining in the area slowed, so did Pioche. But it survived as a small community that today advertises itself as Nevada's "liveliest ghost town."

One hundred seventy-seven miles north of Las Vegas, just west of US 93 off State Highway 322, the mountainside town of Pioche still has numerous nineteenth-century structures built after the town's second disastrous fire, which occurred in 1876. The Pioche Chamber of Commerce (644 Main St.; 775-962-5544) has a Lincoln County guide with driving and walking tours, including a walking tour of Pioche.

Housed in a mercantile building built by A.S. Thompson around 1900 and remodeled in 1929, the **Lincoln County Historical Museum** (63 Main St.; 775-962-5207) features exhibits focusing on the area's earliest American Indian inhabitants and Pioche's boisterous mining boom days.

All on Account of a Jackrabbit?

In 1869 a prospector picked up a rock to throw at a jackrabbit, perhaps thinking the hare might make a meal. But he forgot dinner when he noticed he held a chunk of high-grade silver ore.

At least that's the legend.

No matter how the discovery happened, the mining area around Pioche came to be called the Jackrabbit Mining District. By the time mineral production in the area waned in the 1880s, the district had produced $2 to $6 million in silver.

RENO (WASHOE COUNTY)

Reno got its distinctive name from a railroad official wishing to honor the late Civil War general Jesse Lee Reno, but calling it Fuller or Lake would have been more fitting if less catchy.

In 1859, Charles W. Fuller built a wooden bridge across the Truckee River to accommodate travelers headed to booming Virginia City. Known as Fuller's Crossing, two years later the place became Lake's

Crossing when Fuller sold out to Myron C. Lake, who built a sturdier bridge and opened an inn. He also charged exorbitant tolls—a dollar for a loaded wagon, a half-dollar for a horse and buggy, and a dime for someone on foot. That made Lake good money, but he profited even more by donating land to attract the east-bound Central Pacific Railroad. Extension of an additional rail line from Virginia City to Reno in 1872 boosted the town even more.

Reno's boom lasted until the silver around Virginia City played out, but thanks to its railroad connection the town did well enough until gold and silver mining began around Tonopah and Goldfield at the turn of the twentieth century. As a railroad and mining supply town, Reno became a mecca for those willing to pay for their pleasures or enjoy games of chance. In the early 1900s, the state's liberal divorce laws made it the divorce capital of the nation.

Experience Counted in Indian Fighting

Well before Reno developed, former Texas Ranger Jack Hays led California volunteers in a fight with Paiute Indians on June 2, 1860. Under the leadership of the veteran Indian fighter who had already become legendary, the men routed the warriors along the Truckee River. The engagement, known as the **Second Battle of Pyramid Lake,** came not quite a month after the Paiutes killed forty-six men on the north shore of the lake. The cycle of violence began when a party of miners captured a group of Paiute women to press them into servitude at their camp. The Paiute soon raided the camp to free the women. A force of more than a hundred men then made the mistake of attacking the Indian village. Nearly half of them died in the fight. A Nevada historical marker near the intersection of State Highway 447 and Chicken Road stands on the northern edge of the battlefield site. The battle occurred on what is now the Pyramid Lake Indian Reservation.

The **Nevada Historical Society Museum** (1650 North Virginia Ave.; 775-688-1190) is the state's oldest museum, established in 1904. In addition to historical exhibits, the historical society maintains a large archival collection.

Bonanza Rolling Down the Tracks

The men who robbed the Central Pacific train near Reno on November 4, 1870, figured correctly that the Wells Fargo express car would be carrying a lot of money, but they were wrong in thinking they could get away with their crime. Still, they did succeed in collecting more than $40,000 in gold and silver in the holdup. Unfortunately for them, the giant San Francisco–based transportation company had a large force of detectives on its payroll and soon saturated the area with experienced and well-armed agents. The Wells Fargo men kept their eyes open for big spenders in Reno and soon identified three men who seemed to have a lot of money at their disposal but did not appear to be gainfully employed. On top of that, they evidently knew each other. An agent got one of the men to talk, and soon eight suspects had been arrested. Wells Fargo got most of the loot back and all the participants were convicted, though two were freed for turning state's evidence. Maybe while doing hard labor at the Nevada State Prison, the robbers took at least some satisfaction in knowing that they had committed the first train robbery west of the Mississippi.

A historical marker at Bridge Street and South Verdi Road in Verde (GPS coordinates: N39° 31.05', W119° 59.31') stands at the approximate site of the robbery.

When the Mackay School of Mines opened at the University of Nevada in 1908, a bronze statue of Comstock Lode mining baron John Mackay was placed in front of the school on the main quad of its campus. Gutzon Borglum, the artist whose work appears on Mount Rushmore, sculpted the piece. The statue faces in the direction of Virginia City, where the Irish immigrant Mackay made his fortune.

Mackay's family donated $2 million for the construction of several buildings on campus, including the School of Mines. It is now known as the Mackay School of Earth Sciences and Engineering (1164 Virginia Ave.; 775-784-6987).

RHYOLITE (NYE COUNTY)

On the one-to-ten-scale of mineral hardness developed by German geologist Friedrich Mohs in 1822, the igneous rock known as rhyolite has a rating of six. The mining town of Rhyolite, however, proved far less enduring than its namesake.

In the summer of 1904, the Wild West still not entirely tamed in Nevada, two prospectors found gold-bearing quartz on a hill in the southwestern part of the state. The geologic feature where the high-assaying ore was discovered became known as Bullfrog Hill, and soon, as had happened many times before across the Mountain West, mining camps dotted the high country west of Death Valley.

Soon the larger of those communities was Rhyolite. From a two-man camp in January 1905, by early summer it had 2,500 residents. For a time, the town had more bars, brothels, and gambling joints than it had boardinghouses and eateries. And in a fascinating overlap of old and new transportation technology, the boomtown was served by horse-drawn stagecoaches (four daily to and from Goldfield), three railways, and new-fangled gasoline-powered touring cars.

Before Rhyolite had rail service, building material was hard to come by. An innovative-minded saloonkeeper named Tom Kelly solved that problem in a unique way—he built a three-room house out of glass. As in glass bottles.

With more than two score saloons in town in addition to his own establishment, within six months Kelly had no trouble collecting thousands of clear, brown, and green beer and liquor bottles. Chinking the empties with adobe and plastering the interior walls, he soon had a well-insulated, distinctive-looking house that was an example of recycling at its best long before the term would have its modern meaning.

But for whatever reason, Kelly decided not to live in the house. Instead, at $5 a ticket, he raffled it off. The unique structure almost immediately was labeled by newspapers as "the famous bottle house" and gained national recognition thanks to its appearance on postcards. The winning family lived in the house until 1914, well after Rhyolite had gone into decline. After they left, the bottle house stood vacant for a time before Paramount Pictures repaired it in 1925 when they used the ghost town as a movie set. The films *Wanderers of the Wasteland* and *The Airmail* both featured the unique structure. From 1936 to 1954 the bottle house was operated as a museum. The much-photographed house, one of three bottle houses in Rhyolite, was refurbished in 2005 and still attracts visitors.

Only two years after its founding, Rhyolite was a city with all the conveniences of the early twentieth century: paved sidewalks, public utilities, telephone service, hospitals, an opera—even three swimming pools. Three competing newspapers had no shortage of things to report on, from shootings and killings to the latest mining developments.

Then, as happened time and again in the West, the quality of the gold ore waned, profits plummeted, and the mines began to close. A national recession made the situation even worse. By 1910, having reached an estimated peak population of 10,000, the US Census showed that the town was down to only 611 residents, and barely a decade later, only one elderly man still called Rhyolite home. He died in his nineties in 1924.

What's left of Rhyolite, about a dozen structures in various stages of disrepair, stands on a combination of public land and private property. The more noted and often-photographed ruins include the long-abandoned Spanish-style Las Vegas and Tonopah Railway Depot, the Porter Brothers store, a gutted two-story, eight-room schoolhouse, what's left of the three-story Cook Bank, and an old Union Pacific Railroad caboose someone converted into a house.

The ghost town is just off State Highway 374, four miles west of Beatty, Nevada. The public portions of the ghost town are overseen by the federal Bureau of Land Management, but there is no visitor center or any other amenities at the site.

TONOPAH (NYE COUNTY)

Having completed his term as Nye County district attorney, rancher Jim Butler made camp for the night on his way home to his ranch in Monitor Valley. The next morning, he found a hefty piece of what he thought might be silver ore and collected more samples. Evidently an honest public servant, Butler didn't have enough money to get the rocks assayed. But a lawyer friend (and future Nevada governor) named Tasker Oddie could afford it and agreed to have the ore analyzed in exchange for a piece of the action if the rocks proved to contain silver. The samples tested rich in silver, and Butler and his wife Belle returned to the area and staked their share of three claims. The couple began leasing rights to their claims in 1900 but a year later sold their interests to the Tonopah Mining Company, and yet another Western mining boom began. The town of Tonopah, first named for Butler, grew to ten-thousand-plus, and even though the twentieth century was well under way, the town attracted the usual Wild West characters in search of quick money.

Among those who showed up to capitalize on the boom was Wyatt Earp, who lived with his wife Josie in Tonopah for a time in 1902. Earp had part interest in the Northern Saloon, but also took a lucrative if hard job as a teamster for the Tonopah Mining Company. The former lawman, not yet as famous as he would be, left town after eight months. Built in 1894 in Virginia City, the wood-frame saloon got moved from boomtown to boomtown after Earp and his partner sold out. Since 1998, the privately owned traveling saloon has been in Rancho Mirage, California.

Built in 1907 at the height of the boom, the five-story **Mizpah Hotel** (100 North Main St.; 855-337-3030) was purchased in 2007 by two California winery owners and restored to its original elegance.

In addition to its indoor exhibits on Nye and Esmeralda county history on its grounds, the **Central Nevada Museum** (1900 Logan

Field Rd.; 775-482-9676) features an extensive collection of vintage mining equipment, artifacts, and restored historic buildings.

Operated by a nonprofit foundation, the **Tonopah Mining Park** (110 Burro St.; 775-482-9274) focuses on the history of mining in central Nevada. The park includes original mine shafts, mining equipment, artifacts, and interpretive exhibits. Before the mines played out in the 1930s and early 1940s, the Tonopah Mining District produced five million tons of ore worth $1.2 billion in modern dollars.

VIRGINIA CITY (STOREY COUNTY)

One of the world's richest silver bonanzas, the Comstock Lode brought statehood and growth for Nevada, played a significant role in San Francisco's emergence as a great city, helped finance the US government during the Civil War, expedited the nation's first coast-to-coast telegraph line, and partially bankrolled the first transcontinental railroad. It also made many men incredibly rich, but not those who discovered it.

All the men who had a part in the discovery had come to the western Nevada high country looking for gold, not silver. All had encountered a bluish clay they considered a major impediment in the placer mining of gold. Finally, someone thought to have some of the material assayed and learned it was amazingly rich in silver.

When word spread in California that an almost incomprehensibly rich source of silver had been found in Nevada, in 1859 many prospectors who had rushed west to California to find gold headed east to the new silver diggings. Mining camps developed across the district, but the one that took off was Virginia City. At 6,200 feet along the slope of Mount Davidson, it quickly grew to a major urban center, the business and cultural capital of the Comstock Lode. By 1862, counting nearby Gold Hill, four thousand people lived there. A decade later, the population had reached twenty-five thousand, and Virginia City stood as one of the most important cities between Chicago and the West Coast. The people who lived and worked there came from across the US and the world, particularly Asia. Virginia City had all the amenities and government services of any large city, from fine hotels and opera houses to saloons and bordellos. Officers working in five police precincts and several companies of volunteer firefighters strived to keep the community safe, while several vigorously competing newspapers had no shortage of sensational news to offer readers.

Silver tarnishes and so do silver mining booms. Stunning amounts of silver had come from the lode, but despite a second major discovery in 1872 called the Big Bonanza, by the mid-1870s it began to look like the earth in that part of the world had given up about all it held. Mining slowed and mining jobs decreased. A significant national economic slump in 1874 didn't help, and then a conflagration that even Virginia City's well-organized firefighters couldn't contain blackened much of the community in 1876. As the 1880s began, smelters and the stamp mills that had been breaking down tons of ore to feed them started shutting down.

In only twenty years, from 1860 to 1880, the Comstock Lode had yielded almost seven million tons of ore worth $750 million in 1880 dollars and the equivalent of multiple billions in the twenty-first century. Beyond the wealth it generated, the exploitation of the lode marked the beginning of deep mining in the US, and led to some innovations and operating procedures still in use.

Like other once notable Wild West towns, in the 1950s Virginia City reinvented itself as a tourist destination. As the TV show *Gunsmoke* had done for Dodge City, the popular *Bonanza* series did for Virginia City.

A National Historic Landmark since 1961, the Virginia City Historic District covers 14,750 acres and includes Virginia City plus the smaller mining towns of Gold Hill, Silver City, and Dayton along with numerous mining-related historic sites. Four hundred historic buildings stand within the district. The **Virginia City Visitor Center** (86 C St.; 775-847-7500) has brochures and guidebooks along with self-guided walking tours available in printed format or as smartphone apps.

Virginia City has seventeen museums ranging from traditional to quirky. Museums offering an overview of the Comstock Lode story include the **Courthouse Slammer and County Museum** (26 South B St.; 775-847-0986), and the **Fourth Ward School** (537 South C St.; 775-847-0975). Built in 1876, the four-story schoolhouse was a state-of-the-art nineteenth-century educational facility, complete with indoor flushable toilets. Another general museum is **The Way It Was Museum** (113 C St.; 775-847-0766), a privately owned collection opened in the 1950s. Among numerous more specialized museums are the **Comstock Fire Museum** (125 C St.; 775-847-0717), and the **Comstock Gold Mill** (435 F St.; 800-718-7587), a still-operable historic ore-crushing facility.

Completed in 1869, the **Virginia and Truckee Railroad** (V&T) carried millions of tons of gold and silver ore from the mines around Virginia City to stamping mills in Carson City. The line remained in operation until 1950.

Since 2009, a reconstituted V&T has been running trains between Virginia City and Carson City (along with a Virginia City to Gold Hill route). V&T rolling stock includes two restored steam locomotives, a diesel locomotive, and vintage passenger cars. Tickets are available online at https://vtrailway.com or at the restored 1870 V&T Depot (166 F St.). Near the depot is the **Comstock History Center** (20 North E St.; 775-847-0419). Despite its generic name, the center is a reconstructed railroad car shed that houses Dayton No. 19, a vintage V&T locomotive, as well as exhibits relating to the historic rail line.

Built in 1860, the two-story brick **Mackay Mansion** (291 South D St.) is named for its famous short-term resident, John Mackay. The Irish-born millionaire and philanthropist, one of the lode's four so-called Silver Kings, lived there only a few months, as did James Fair, another of the kings. George Hearst, father of future newspaper baron William Randolph Hearst, built the mansion. Initially it served as headquarters for the Gould and Curry Mining Co. and the superintendent's residence. The mansion is privately owned but open for tours and rentable for special events.

The *Territorial Enterprise*

Mark Twain was "born" while Samuel Clemens reported for Virginia City's feisty and often wildly sensational *Territorial Enterprise*. Clemens first used the pen name "Josh," but soon switched to the *nom de plume* that would become known worldwide as he evolved from journalist to novelist, essayist, and lecturer.

The building that housed the newspaper during Twain's time on the staff no longer stands, but the newspaper occupied a two-story brick building (23 South C St.) in 1876 that has survived. For many years, the building housed a museum displaying hot-metal newspaper equipment and related artifacts along with a desk Twain supposedly used while writing for the *Enterprise*.

Though "cemetery" is a singular noun, **Silver Terrace Cemetery** (381 Cemetery Rd.)—established in 1867 when graves were moved from Virginia City's first cemetery—actually is a collection of eleven diverse sections, from a Masonic cemetery to a section reserved for "Exempt Firemen." That means retired firefighters.

The cemetery complex is located northeast of town off Carson Street. A brochure pointing out interesting graves is available at the cemetery's entrance or at the visitor center. The most imposing monument in the cemetery honors county namesake Edward Faris Storey (1829–1860), a Georgia-born Indian fighter who died in action against a Paiute party near Pyramid Lake, Nevada, on June 2, 1860. The monument was erected in 1930.

WINNEMUCCA (HUMBOLDT COUNTY)

Winnemucca, named for a storied Paiute chief, began as a trading post at a crossing of the Humboldt River used by west-bound travelers on the Oregon Trail. Mining in the area perked up the community's economy in the early 1860s, and the arrival of the Central Pacific Railroad further assured the town vitality.

The **Winnemucca Hotel** (95 Bridge St.) is the town's oldest building. The **Humboldt County Museum** (175 Museum Ln.; 775-623-2912) occupies the 1907 St. Mary's Episcopal Church. The old house of worship was moved to the site and restored in 1977.

Somebody Robbed the Bank, But Who?

Three men robbed the First National Bank of Winnemucca on September 19, 1900, but one of them was not Robert LeRoy Parker, alias Butch Cassidy. (That's because Parker is known to have been planning a train robbery in Wyoming at the time.) Whether the other two men belonged to the Wild Bunch has remained a matter of debate for generations, but the consensus is that they were not. Whoever the robbers were, they remained at-large, and their $30,000-plus haul was never recovered.

The two-story building once occupied by the bank still stands on the northwest corner of Fourth and Bridge Streets, Winnemucca.

YERINGTON (LYON COUNTY)

In the fertile Mason Valley along the Walker River, Yerington started as a farm and ranch community in the mid-nineteenth century and gained momentum when copper mining began in the area in the twentieth century. The first settler was Hock Mason, who while on his way to California in 1857 decided he needn't go farther and began raising cattle in the valley. When the Carson & Colorado Railroad reached the town in 1890, it became a supply center and agricultural shipping point. Prospectors found copper ore in the Singaste Mountains west of Yerington in 1911, and copper mining surpassed agriculture as the town's principal economic force until the last mine closed in 1978.

The **Lyon County Museum** (215 South Main; 775-463-6576) focuses on the history of the Yerington area.

Fort Churchill

Established in July 1860 on the north bank of the Carson River to protect overland travelers, miners, and the Pony Express, **Fort Churchill** was Nevada's first military installation and became its largest. Its troops also guarded and maintained the transcontinental telegraph line within the fort's area of responsibility and participated in several Indian Wars engagements. The fort was abandoned in 1869.

Since 1957 the ruins of the fort have been the primary attraction at **Fort Churchill State Historic Park** (10000 US 95A, Silver Springs; 775-577-2345), thirty-two miles north of Yerington; http://parks.nv.gov/parks/fort-churchill.

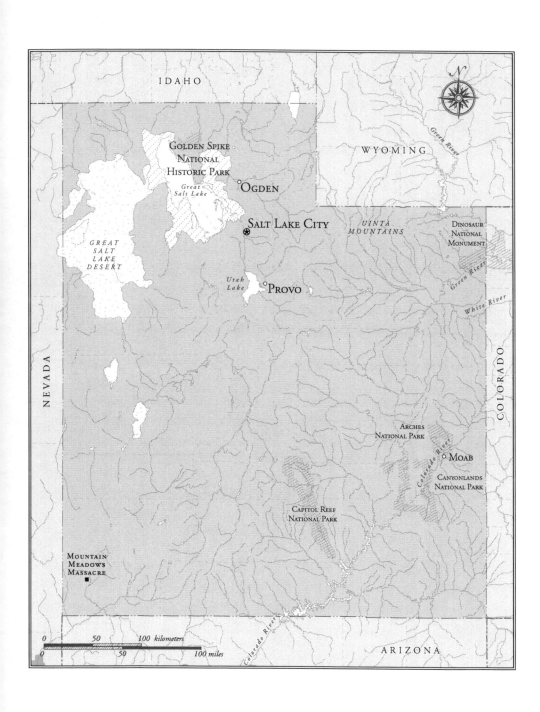

UTAH

Beaver (Beaver County)

Mormon pioneers settled Beaver, named for nearby Beaver Creek, in 1856. Ten years later, one of the Wild West's most notorious outlaws was born there, but not under the name most people recognize.

The firstborn son of Mormon emigrants, Robert LeRoy Parker was born in Beaver in 1866 and spent his first thirteen or so years in the Beaver River Valley. His family's hired hand, Mike Cassidy, tutored the youth in the fine art of horse stealing and cattle rustling. Leaving home as a teenager, Robert soon began calling himself George Cassidy. After embarking on a career of outlawry, he became far better known as Butch Cassidy. The Parker family residence no longer stands, but the 1882 **Beaver Courthouse Museum** (90 East Center St.; 435-438-5727) has a Butch Cassidy exhibit along with exhibits on the history of the town and the county.

The US Army established Fort Cameron in 1872 two miles east of Beaver, and while the community appreciated the protection it afforded and the assistance of the military in providing security for the January 26, 1878, execution of Mountain Meadows Massacre participant John D. Lee, the Mormons did not like the saloons and bordellos that catered to the soldiers. The post was abandoned in 1883. The town continued as an agricultural community.

Beaver has more than a hundred nineteenth-century structures. The Beaver County Travel Council (400 South Main St.; 435-438-6482) has a self-guided tour of local historic sites.

Fort Cove

In 1867 Brigham Young tasked Ira Hinckley to build a fort on Cove Creek on the road between Salt Lake and the former territorial capital at Fillmore. Hinckley saw to the construction of a one-hundred-foot-square, volcanic rock and timber fortification, and for a decade lived there and provided travelers with shelter and other necessities. Later, **Fort Cove** became part of a ranching operation, but descendants of Hinckley bought the land in 1988 and donated it to the Latter-day Saints for restoration. The fort is just northeast of the junction of I-15 and I-70, twenty-four miles north of Beaver on State Highway 161; (435) 438-5547.

BRIGHAM CITY (BOX ELDER COUNTY)

The area around what would become Brigham City was first settled by Mormons in 1851, though the town named for Brigham Young was not laid out until 1855. While Brigham City has ample history related to the Mormon settlement of Utah, an event that took place a day's horseback ride to the west of the town was a pivotal moment in the nation's history.

Golden Spike National Historic Site

Considering the first transcontinental rail line's enduring impact, the point where tracks from the east first met tracks from the west only four years after the Civil War is viewed by many scholars as the most significant historic site west of Philadelphia's Independence Hall.

In May 1869, as the two tracks progressed toward their joining (an event that came to be called the "Wedding of the Rails"), white canvas tents bloomed in the Utah desert. The tents sheltered railroad workers, telegraphers, contractors, the Wells Fargo agent, and others. The next row of tents, located across the right-of-way from the first row, were saloons and eateries.

On May 10, with the Central Pacific's locomotive Jupiter facing the Union Pacific's Engine No. 119, a solid gold spike was ceremoniously driven to mark the momentous occasion. The event was captured in one of the West's most iconic photographs.

Promontory City, everyone believed, was destined to become a prosperous railroad junction. More tents sprang up, soon to be replaced by more permanent business buildings and residences. But railroad officials decided that Ogden, Utah, would be the transfer and maintenance point, and by December 1869 Promontory City had disappeared.

Not counting the length of time that a transcontinental railroad had been discussed and planned, completing the coast-to-coast rail connection took six years. But nearly a century passed before Congress created the **Golden Spike National Historical Park** (435-471-2209) in 1965. By the time the centennial of the "Wedding of the Rails" ceremony was observed in 1969, a visitor center with exhibits telling the story had been opened. On the 110th anniversary, two operable replicas of the famous steam locomotives added to the visitor experience. An estimated one hundred thousand people took part in the three-day 150th anniversary event in May 2019. The national historical park is thirty-two miles west of Brigham City on State Highway 83.

Founded in 1970, the **Brigham City Museum of Art and History** (24 North 300 West; 435-226-1439) focuses on the history of the city as well as art, with standing and rotating exhibits. **Anderson Wagon Land Adventures** (8790 West 11200 North, Tremonton; 435-279-6422) has a collection of some 350 restored horse-drawn vehicles.

Cedar City (Iron County)

Most Old West mining operations extracted silver, gold, or copper, but a different element spurred settlement of this area—iron. Following the discovery of rich iron ore deposits in this vicinity, Brigham Young sent missionaries to establish an iron works and foundry. First called Little Muddy, then Coal Creek, and finally Cedar City, the community was a pig iron production center from 1852 to 1858.

It might have become the Pittsburgh of the West, but the area was prone to flooding, there were problems with the coal-fueled furnace, and relations were not good with the American Indians who had used this part of the West for hundreds of years. Still, before the last blast-furnace fire was banked, some twenty-five tons of iron had been produced here.

The town survived the loss of its iron works and saw another effort fail in the 1870s, but iron ore mining continued around it well into the twentieth century.

Established in 1973 and originally known as Iron Mission State Park, **Frontier Homestead State Park** (635 North Main St.; 435-586-9290) tells the story of Iron County, from its early iron production days through the 1920s. Among the many artifacts on display may be the only surviving product made at the early foundry, the town bell. The park also showcases the Gronway Parry Collection of old horse-drawn vehicles, including buggies, wagons, sleighs, and stagecoaches. One of the stagecoaches has bullet holes in it, lingering evidence of an early-day holdup or Indian attack. **Old Iron Town Historic Site,** the second Cedar City area iron works, is twenty-five miles west of Cedar City at 4128 South 17800 West, off State Highway 56.

CIRCLEVILLE (PIUTE COUNTY)

For years, it was just an old log cabin in rural Piute County, interesting as a surviving piece of frontier architecture, but certainly no tourist destination. Then came the 1969 movie *Butch Cassidy and the Sundance Kid*. Suddenly, an all-but-forgotten late nineteenth-century outlaw gang gained national and international prominence. The slowly deteriorating cabin where Robert LeRoy Parker (aka Butch Cassidy) spent much of his childhood became an oft-visited attraction, even though it stands on private property. In 2016, the Utah legislature appropriated $138,000 for the cabin's disassembly and restoration. Privately raised funding also went into the project, which in addition to stabilizing the cabin included construction of a parking lot, picnic tables, and restrooms as well as interpretive signage developed by the Utah Division of State Parks.

The cabin is three miles south of Circleville off US 89 between Richfield and Panquitch. While the structure is only open to the public for special events, it can be viewed from the outside.

Fillmore (Millard County)

When Congress created Utah Territory in 1850, newly appointed governor Brigham Young wanted the capital located in the center of the future state, nearly 150 miles south of Salt Lake City. Since President Millard Fillmore had appointed him, Young named the new capital in his honor. Construction soon began on what was projected to be a large, imposing statehouse, but only one wing had been completed by 1858 when the territorial legislature voted to move the seat of government to Salt Lake. The old capitol, a two-story stone building that looks more like an old county courthouse than a capitol, became Utah's first state park in 1957. **Territorial Statehouse State Park** (50 West Capitol Ave.; 435-743-5316) preserves the state's oldest government building and the grounds around it. In addition to interpreting the history of the building, the museum focuses on what pioneer life was like in Utah.

Thirty-six miles northwest of Fillmore, the **Great Basin Museum** (45 West Main St., Delta; 435-864-5013) focuses on the history of Millard County.

Frisco (Beaver County)

With the opening of the Horn Silver Mine in 1875—one of the richest in the West—Frisco (named for nearby San Francisco Peak) came into being. Quickly becoming a community of some six thousand with all the attendant boomtown rowdiness, Frisco flourished until early 1885, when a cave-in likely triggered by a minor earthquake caused the mine to close for a lengthy period and collapsed the local economy. Like so many other Western mining towns, Frisco was soon abandoned, though mining continued in the area until the 1920s. At its peak the mine produced 150 tons of ore a day.

Ruins of the old mining town are 14.4 miles northwest of Milford, Utah, off State Highway 21. The most unique remnants of the ghost town are five beehive-shaped granite charcoal kilns (charcoal was integral to the ore smelting process), now listed on the National

Register of Historic Places (GPS coordinates: N38° 27.62', W113° 15.78').

GREEN RIVER (EMERY COUNTY)

The Green River is the largest tributary of the Colorado, and the town of Green River developed at a river crossing that had been used for generations. Settlement began in 1876 around a stagecoach stop known as Blake Station, but the community did not grow much until the Utah Division of the Denver and Rio Grande Railroad arrived in 1883 and opened a depot there. That made Green River a supply and shipping point, which attracted prospectors, cowboys, and outlaws. The Denver and Rio Grande's 1892 decision to move most of its facilities to Helper stunted the town's growth.

John Wesley Powell (1834–1902), the famed one-armed explorer of the Colorado River and Grand Canyon in 1869, also made two trips down the Green River. The first was undertaken the same year he explored the Colorado. The second Green River trip was in 1871. Powell's expeditions, coming six decades after Lewis and Clark blazed their trail across the West, opened up the last great uncharted area of the continental US.

The twenty-three-thousand-square-foot **John Wesley Powell River History Museum** (1765 East Main St.; 435-564-3427) opened in 1990. Operated by the City of Green River and a nonprofit group, the museum has exhibits and research material related to Powell, a collection of vintage boats, and displays on the history of the Green River area.

HELPER (CARBON COUNTY)

Founded in 1881 following the arrival of the Denver and Rio Grande Railroad, Helper got its unusual name from the powerful helper engines that assisted trains in making it up a steep grade nearby. The town flourished as a railroad division point and coal mining center. On April 21, 1897, Butch Cassidy and Elzy Lay robbed three employees of the Pleasant Valley Coal Company near the nearby Castle Gate railroad depot and escaped with roughly $8,000 in gold.

Located in the old Helper Hotel (built 1913–1914), the **Western Mining and Railroad Museum** (296 South Main St.; 435-472-3009) focuses on the two primary factors in the development of the area—coal mining and the railroad. Emigrants from more than twenty-seven countries came to this area for mining jobs during the period of peak production from 1880 to 1950. The museum also has a display related to the Wild Bunch.

LOGAN (CACHE COUNTY)

Where mountain men rendezvoused in the 1820s, a group of Mormons established a farming community on the Logan River in 1859. The town, later named for a Mormon elder, became home of the state's land-grant college, an institution that became Utah State University.

Logan was an exceedingly tame town by Wild West standards, but since the mid-1990s visitors have been able to get a feel for what the West was like at the **American West Heritage Center** (4025 South US 89/91, Wellsville; 435-245-6050). Ten miles southwest of Logan, the center is jointly operated by a nonprofit foundation and Utah State University. It has exhibits that focus on the 1820 to 1920 period and offers a wide range of living-history programs.

MOAB (GRAND COUNTY)

At a natural crossing of the Colorado River, Moab began in the spring of 1855 as a Mormon trading post called Elk Mountain Mission, but frequent Indian attacks led to its abandonment that fall. Permanent settlement did not come until 1878, and the town was not incorporated until 1902. Initially an agricultural center, Moab benefited from mining activity in the area, but the Denver and Rio Grande Railroad bypassed it in 1883.

Founded in 1957, the **Moab Museum** (118 East Center St.; 435-259-7985) focuses on the cultural and natural history of the area. By the 1980s the museum had more exhibits and artifacts than it had room for, and planning for a new building began. That building opened in 1988, and a major remodeling project was completed in 2020. In addition to its displays, the museum has a large archival collection. The **Moab Museum of Film and Western Heritage** (Red Cliffs Ranch, Milepost 14, State Highway 128; 866-812-2002) explores the area's long connection to the movie-making industry.

Dead Horse Point State Park may not have the most inviting name, but there's an interesting story behind it. The centerpiece of the park is a rocky point that towers two thousand feet over a bend in the Colorado River. Supposedly, early ranchers in the area drove wild horses to the point and then piled brush on the narrow neck leading to it so as to corral the mustangs on the point. For reasons not explained in the legend, the horses were abandoned and ended up starving to death. The 5,362-acre park is thirty-two miles from Moab. Take US 191 northwest from Moab for nine miles, then turn left on State Highway 313 and drive twenty-three miles to the park. A visitor center (435-259-2614) has interpretive exhibits on natural and cultural history.

For additional spectacular scenery and interesting history, visit **Arches National Park** (435-719-2299) and **Canyonlands National Park** (435-719-2313). For Arches, drive five miles north from Moab on US 191 and turn right at the stoplight. Canyonlands has four districts, each reached a different way. Visit the park's website for the best routes.

Monument Valley (Navajo Nation)

The spectacular geology of Monument Valley—nearly ninety-two thousand acres of variously shaped towering red sandstone formations—is not found anywhere else in the world. Most of the valley, a stunning expanse of spires, buttes, and rocky arches that straddles the Utah-Arizona border, lies within the twenty-seven-thousand-square-mile Navajo reservation and is included in **Monument Valley Navajo Tribal Park.**

Portions of the park, which the Navajo established in 1958, have petroglyphs dating back thousands of years, and a few score Navajo live on the desert floor in huts lacking electricity or water, but Euro-Americans considered the area too desolate for settlement, especially after it became apparent that it had no precious-metal deposits. The officer in charge of the first detachment of US soldiers to explore the area reported that it was "as desolate and repulsive looking a country as can be imagined."

In 1868, the federal government established a reservation for the Navajo nearby, but the valley and its distinctive landscape remained public land until the reservation was expanded to include most of it in 1933. Under Navajo control, the valley was safe from exploitation, but not far from the reservation a real estate transaction that took place twelve years earlier would change the way the world envisioned the Old West.

In 1921, Henry Goulding and his wife Leone (nicknamed "Mike") paid $320 for 640 acres adjoining Monument Valley, just north of the Arizona border in Utah. Living in one tent and using another tent for their planned commercial enterprise, the Gouldings opened a trading post catering to the Navajo. The couple soon earned the trust and respect of the Navajo people, and by 1927 the Gouldings could afford to start construction of a two-story, cut sandstone trading post. Their store was on the ground level, and they lived upstairs.

Two years later the economy collapsed as the nation entered the Great Depression. A bad drought and the consequences of overgrazing on the reservation made things even worse. Then one day in 1938 the Gouldings heard on the radio that Hollywood was looking for a good location to film a Western. Packing their bedrolls and camping gear, the couple drove to California with an assortment of black-and-white photos showing the valley's unique terrain.

At United Artists, an overzealous receptionist refused to let the Gouldings see anyone. The studio official who showed up to throw them out saw one of the photos and realized the couple might be worth listening to. Soon, Goulding was giving director John Ford a photographic tour of the valley and its otherworldly landscape. Ford realized the area would make a stunning backdrop for a Western and sent the Gouldings back to Utah with a $5,000 check. The Depression for the couple was over—their trading post would be the California film crew's base of operations.

The movie Ford directed there was *Stagecoach*. Starring a young actor named John Wayne, the Western won an Academy Award and launched Wayne's career. Ford went on to shoot five more movies in Monument Valley, and several score film and television productions have been filmed in the valley since then.

As far as theatergoers were concerned, the Westerns that Ford and other directors filmed in Monument Valley depicted the landscape of Arizona, New Mexico, Texas, or some other southwestern state. But for millions of people, the unique southern Utah landscape became synonymous with the West.

Still in operation, **Goulding's Trading Post** (1000 Goulding Trading Post Rd.; 435-727-3231) now includes a hotel and a museum focused on the valley as a movie-making mecca.

OGDEN (WEBER COUNTY)

Utah's oldest city, Ogden was settled in 1846 by mountain man Miles Goodyear. Selecting a site just east of a bend in the Weber River a couple of miles downstream from its confluence with the Ogden River, Goodyear built a trading post he called Fort Buenaventura. Only thirty-five miles to the south, Mormon leader Brigham Young did not like the idea of a "Gentile" community so near his, and eventually Mormon settler James Brown bought Goodyear's property and livestock for $2,000. Any hope the Mormons had of keeping non-Mormons out of Utah died with the arrival of the first transcontinental railroad in 1869, and Ogden grew as a major railway center.

A reconstruction of Goodyear's cabin and trading post stands on its original site in **Fort Buenaventura Park** (2450 A Ave.; 801-399-8099), initially a state park but later transferred to Weber County. In nearby Miles Goodyear Park is Goodyear's original log cabin and a museum telling the story of Ogden's settlement and development.

Built in 1924, Ogden's Union Station (2501 Wall Ave.; 801-629-8680) used to be a busy place. With the steady arrival and departure of coast-to-coast passenger trains, the Ogden Chamber of Commerce boasted that a traveler couldn't get anywhere without going to Ogden first. The passenger trains are gone, but the station is home to three museums relating to the Old West: The **Utah State Railroad Museum,** the **John M. Browning Firearms Museum,** and the **Utah Cowboy Western Heritage Museum.**

PARK CITY (SUMMIT COUNTY)

A mining town in the Wasatch Mountains dating to the 1860s, Park City was a near ghost town until development of the ski industry in the early 1950s gave it new life. Though a fire destroyed much of the town in 1898, several of its historic structures survived. The town gained further traction in 1978 with the founding of the annual Sundance Film Festival, and even more when it hosted the 2002 Winter Olympics. The **Park City Historical Museum** (528 Main St.; 435-649-7457) is in the old city hall (which included a territorial jail), built for $6,400 in 1885–1886.

Built in 1886 and a survivor of the devastating fire that broke out twelve years later, the wood-frame **Union Pacific Depot** railroad station (600 Main St.; 435-649-7457) continued in operation until 1977. Later, in 1995, actor Robert Redford renovated the building, which looked more like a Victorian mansion than a railroad station. It housed a restaurant and other businesses.

One of the few Utah communities not established by Mormons, during its peak mining boom days, Park City supported twenty-seven saloons and other even less savory establishments. And like most wide-open towns, killings were not rare. But most of the time, the citizenry took murders in stride. For instance, when gambling man Henry Nugent killed Peter Clark at Riley and Towey's Gambling Hall, folks considered it a fair fight. Nor did any of the townspeople get particularly exercised when Fred Hopt killed his old friend John Turner with an axe during a Fourth of July celebration. Everyone knew they didn't get along. But when popular miner Matthew Brannan fell off his horse, mortally wounded by a bullet fired from ambush by Black Jack Murphy, that was considered way out of bounds. Murphy wisely turned himself in before a lynch mob could form, but local authorities did not think they could forestall vigilante action for long and secretly moved the prisoner to the county seat at Coalville, twenty-four miles to the north. When word of Murphy's location got out, a group of miners seized a locomotive, rounded up a train crew, forced them to attach a car to accommodate passengers, and ordered the "special" to take them to Coalville. There they collected Murphy without incident. When the train got back to Park City, the delegation duly conducted a trial at the depot. Meanwhile, confident in the impartial administration of justice, others in the mob draped a rope over the cross arm of a telephone pole.

Contemporary news accounts said Murphy's lynching occurred "at the foot of Main Street" near the depot. The **Kimball Art Center** (1401 Kearns Blvd.) stands at the approximate location, though the telephone pole is long gone and there is no marker. A local ghost tour stops at the site. The location of Murphy's grave is not known, but he is believed to have been buried in the Park City Cemetery, either in an unmarked grave or beneath a long-since decayed wooden marker. Brannan received an elaborate funeral, the procession to the cemetery led by a band, and was buried beneath a white marble marker that has since broken in half.

The Strawberry Bandits

So far as is known, only once in Wild West history did the theft of strawberries lead to murder. Two killings, in fact. On July 11, 1895, a Massachusetts-born Irish rowdy named Patrick Coughlin stole six cases of strawberries from a Park City vendor. He and a confederate, Fred George, planned to sell them to the madam of one of the town's bawdy houses.

The vendor readily identified the pair, and Sheriff John Harrigan swore out a warrant and set out with a deputy to arrest the thieves. The lawmen trailed the strawberry bandits to a remote canyon north of town where, after an exchange of gunfire, the petty thieves-turned-outlaws escaped. The pair made it to Rich County, Utah, and holed up in an abandoned cabin in Echo Canyon. When a rancher discovered their hideout, he notified Echo City constable Thomas Stagg in adjacent Summit County, who organized a posse and surrounded the cabin on July 30, 1895.

In the shootout that followed, Stagg and posse member Edward Dawes were killed. The other posse members backed off, and the killers made their getaway. Finally arrested near Grantsville, Utah, close to the Nevada border, the pair were tried and convicted. George got a life sentence while Coughlin was sentenced to death. He was executed by firing squad on December 15, 1896.

Under a white marble tombstone bearing only his name and date of birth and death, Coughlin is buried in the family plot in the southwest corner of **Glenwood Cemetery** (401 Silver King Dr.). Constable Stagg (1833–1895) is buried in **Echo Historical Cemetery,** near the intersection of South Echo Road and Dwight D. Eisenhauer Highway (GPS coordinates: N40° 58.73', W111° 26.48').

PRICE CITY (CARBON COUNTY)

Price City began as a ranching community in 1877 but boomed as a coal mining town in 1883. The **Carbon County Visitor Center** (751 East 100 North; 435-636-3701) has maps and brochures on area historic sites and other attractions.

A twenty-five-year-old Texan way off his range, Joe Walker turned to outlawry in Utah and became part of Butch Cassidy's gang in the mid-1890s. He had started off in a good family, but his father was killed by Indians in Arizona. When his mother became a widow, she moved to Utah and turned management of her cattle herd over to her brother. Following her death, when Walker sought his share of the cattle, his uncle refused to acknowledge him. While that likely soured him on life, he first got on the wrong side of the law when he got drunk and shot up the town in Price in 1895. He fled town and before long ended up in the Wild Bunch. Though he specialized in rustling, he is believed to have participated in the April 21, 1897, Castle Gate, Utah, robbery. Walker had a couple of "gunsmokey" close calls with officers, but on May 13, 1898, a posse finally caught up with him and a colleague near Thompson Springs, some ninety miles southeast of Price. Depending on the source, Walker and the other man either died in a shootout with the lawmen or were shot to death by posse members as they lay asleep in their bedrolls. At first the officers believed they had killed Cassidy as well as Walker, but it turned out to be a man named Joe Herring.

Nearly a century after Joe Walker's violent demise, federal Bureau of Land Management archaeologists discovered a tombstone bearing the outlaw's name and a date of death in 1897. Trouble was, it is well documented that Walker did not die until 1898. When the archaeologists excavated beneath the marker, they hit solid rock only a few inches down. Later, a second phony Joe Walker tombstone was found. It's only an educated guess, but the archaeologists surmised that Walker placed the fake markers hoping to convince law enforcement that he was dead.

Being outlaws, Walker and Herring were buried outside the fence surrounding the **Price City Cemetery** (595 East 400 North; section P, plot 32, lot 4) so as not to be in the same company with the good people laid to rest inside the fence. But in the 1970s, the city expanded the cemetery, and the remains of the two men, along with a third set belonging to an American Indian who had also been excluded from the cemetery proper, were reinterred. Even so, the relocation did not amount to any change in status for Walker and Herring. While now inside the cemetery, their new graves are in a section reserved for outlaws.

Robber's Roost

The more successful outlaws knew when, and usually where, to make themselves scarce following the commission of a crime. Butch Cassidy and his colleagues liked to get lost in the harsh high desert terrain of Capitol Reef in southeastern Utah in an area that became known as **Robber's Roost.** It is still remote and hard to get to, but when they see the area's steep-walled canyons and draws, those who do go there will certainly appreciate that the area made for a great hideout. Lawmen hunting the Wild Bunch never successfully penetrated Robber's Roost.

From Hanksville travel north on State Highway 24 to Robber's Roost Trail, a twenty-eight-mile stretch of unpaved road best for four-wheel-drive or other off-road vehicles. Trails lead from the Robber's Roost site parking area to various points of historical interest, including the Butch Cassidy cabin (GPS coordinates: N38° 21.40', W110° 21.57').

PROVO (WASATCH COUNTY)

In March 1849, Brigham Young sent 150 colonists to settle in the Utah Valley along the Provo River, a stream named for Etienne Provost, a Frenchman who established a trading post near Utah Lake in the mid-1820s. The new arrivals built a log fort just south of the stream a couple of miles above Utah Lake, but moved a year later to higher ground and constructed a second fortification. Called Fort Utah, it consisted of a fourteen-foot stockade enclosing a cluster of cabins. American Indians living in the valley rightfully viewed the arrival of the Mormons as an incursion, and hostilities soon developed. Periodic warfare continued in the area for nearly a decade, but the town of Provo was incorporated in 1851 and continued to grow as an agricultural center. An educational institution called Brigham Young Academy was founded in 1875 and later became Brigham Young University.

Provo has two museums focused on the town and surrounding area: the **BYU Museum of Peoples and Cultures** (2201 North Canyon Rd.; 801-422-0020) and **Provo Pioneer Village** (600 North 500 West; 801-375-9299).

RICHFIELD (SEVIER COUNTY)

Mormon pioneers settled this community in 1864, naming it for the fertile soil they found. When the Black Hawk War broke out the following year, three of the ten pioneers who had built a large dugout there were killed. The place was abandoned in 1867 and no one returned until 1871. After the Denver and Rio Grande Railroad came through in 1891, Richfield grew as a farming and ranching town.

Thirty-eight years before the first settlers arrived, famed mountain man Jedediah Strong Smith traveled through Clear Creek Canyon, twenty-one miles south of future Richfield. As related in the journal he kept, Smith was trapping beaver along Clear Creek in the fall of 1826 on his expedition to California. On that trek, which had begun in August that year and continued through early July 1827, Smith discovered what came to be called South Pass, a passage across the Continental Divide that saw heavy use during the later heyday of the Oregon Trail.

In 2016, a monument commemorating Smith was placed in **Fremont Indian State Park** (3820 West Clear Creek Canyon Rd., Sevier; 435-527-4631). The monument and interpretive signage is two miles east of the park visitor center and museum.

ST. GEORGE (WASHINGTON COUNTY)

St. George is more than 1,500 miles from the heart of Mississippi cotton-growing country, but for a time the community was known as "Little Dixie." That's because Mormon leader Brigham Young dispatched families to southwestern Utah at the beginning of the Civil War to grow cotton and silkworms in anticipation of diminished supplies of textiles because of the Union naval blockade of the South. The settlers didn't succeed in cotton cultivation, but they did well growing fruit, including grapes.

The St. George Area Chamber of Commerce (136 North 100 East; 435-628-1658) has a self-guided walking tour of the downtown historic district and other historic sites. The **Daughters of Utah Pioneer Museum** (145 North 100 East; 435-628-7274) has exhibits on the history of St. George and Washington County.

Excluding bloodletting related to the Civil War or Indian warfare, the Mountain Meadows Massacre claimed more lives than in any other mass killing west of the Mississippi in the nineteenth century. An estimated 120 to 140 men, women, and children died when a Mormon militia force and some Paiute Indians attacked a wagon train on its way from Arkansas to California. Most of the deaths came on September 11, 1857, though the wagon train was first attacked on September 7. The factors that led to the attack have continued to be debated into the twenty-first century, but not its brutality.

US troops went to the massacre site two years later and buried the remains they found, covering the mass grave with a cairn supporting a cedar cross. In 1864 the original monument was destroyed by Mormons and the army replaced it. A short stone wall was built around the monument in 1932 and a modern **Mountain Meadows Massacre Monument** erected at the site in 1999. In 2011 the scene of the massacre was designated as a National Historic Landmark. The site is thirty-five miles north of St. George on State Highway 18.

SALT LAKE CITY (SALT LAKE COUNTY)

Mormon pioneers founded Salt Lake City in July 1847. Led by Brigham Young, they were the initial Anglos to settle in the Salt Lake Valley. The first contingent of settlers was not large, only 143 men, three women, and two children. Other Mormons ventured to the new settlement, but life was not easy. Bad weather and a cricket infestation nearly destroyed all the crops in 1848, but flocks of seagulls devoured the insects, and the settlers were able to harvest enough to make it through the winter of 1848–49. Salt Lake became a supply point during the California gold rush. Still part of Mexico when the Mormons arrived, the settlement came under US control in 1850 and Utah was made a territory. The arrival of the transcontinental railroad in 1869 connected Salt Lake with the rest of the nation, and as the state capital and world headquarters for the Church of Latter-day Saints, it grew steadily as Utah's largest city.

This Is the Place

Looking down on the Salt Lake Valley from the mouth of Emigrant Canyon in the foothills of the Wasatch Mountains with his Church of Latter-day Saints followers, Brigham Young said four words, "This is the place." And indeed, it proved to be. **This Is the Place Heritage Park** (2601 Sunnyside Ave.; 801-582-1847) is a collection of restored and re-created historic structures making up a pioneer village that gives a sense of what Salt Lake City was first like.

Now a National Historic Landmark, Brigham Young built what came to be called the **Beehive House** (67 East South Temple St.; 801-240-2681) in 1854, seven years after he and his followers founded Salt Lake City. Next door is the Lion House, which Young constructed to accommodate his twenty-seven wives and fifty-six children. The second president of the Latter-day Saints, Young served as Utah's first governor.

Established in 1862 as Camp Douglas, the post was critical in the US government's successful effort to prevent Mormon-dominated Utah Territory from joining the Confederate cause. At a time when President Lincoln feared Washington, DC, would be invaded, 20 percent of the US Army was stationed in Utah. Maintaining federal control of Utah was that important. The camp became Fort Douglas in 1878 and continued as an active military garrison until 1991. Located in one of the post's nineteenth-century buildings, the **Fort Douglas**

Military Museum (32 Potter St.; 801-581-1251) opened in 1976 and has since been expanded.

One of the Wild West's more eccentric characters ended up in Salt Lake. Joseph Alfred "Jack" Slade (1829–1864), the son of a lawmaker from Illinois, found it expedient to go west after killing a man in his home state. In Colorado Territory he operated a stagecoach station. When he had a falling out with Jules Beni (namesake of Julesburg), he killed him and cut off his ears, one of which he carried for a time on his watch chain. But in Virginia City, Montana, where vigilantes had undertaken to create a more law-abiding community, a drunken spree ended with Slade receiving a "suspended" sentence. Following the March 10, 1864, lynching, Slade's widow came to town and had his body placed in a lead-lined, alcohol-filled coffin. Though the alcohol was fitting enough, its purpose was to keep the body preserved long enough for burial in Salt Lake. Slade's grave is in **Salt Lake City Cemetery** (200 North St. East; 801-596-5020; block B, lot 6, grave 7).

Andrew H. Burk, Salt Lake's city marshal, seldom carried a pistol. A big man, he generally found a few well-placed whacks with his walking stick gained the cooperation of someone unwilling to be arrested or settle down. But when Burk answered a disturbance call at a downtown restaurant, Sam Harvey shot the marshal with a rifle. Burk staggered to a nearby drugstore and soon died. A mob formed outside city hall, and despite the efforts of officers and jailers, a rope was put around Harvey's neck and he was dragged down the street to a livery stable where he was summarily lynched. Only twenty-five minutes had elapsed since the time of Burk's shooting to Harvey's hanging.

An engraved bronze plaque bearing Burk's photo and details of his last watch was placed on the **Walker Center** (200 South and Main Street)—the scene of the marshal's killing—in 2011. Present for the unveiling was the chief's great-great-grandson, a retired Salt Lake police lieutenant. The Scottish-born Burk (1828–1883) lies beneath a tall granite tombstone in Salt Lake City Cemetery (block A, lot 1, grave 2).

Operated by the Daughters of Utah Pioneers, the six-floor **Pioneer Memorial Museum** (300 North Main St.; 801-532-6479) tells the story of the Mormon trek from Illinois to what they saw as the promised land, present-day Utah. In addition to exhibits and artifacts dealing with the history of Mormon settlement, there are more eclectic Western-related items on display, including a set of Buddhist scrolls brought by one of the multiple thousands of Chinese who helped build railroads, worked in mines, or otherwise played a part in the area's economy and culture.

SILVER REEF (WASHINGTON COUNTY)

Silver does not occur in sandstone—except when it does. Conventional wisdom to the contrary, in the early 1870s prospectors discovered silver oxide–bearing sandstone in a geologic formation in southern Utah known as the White Reef. Soon a town that came to be called Silver Reef arose near the new play. A strike by miners in 1881 sent the bustling town into decline, and when the bottom fell out of the silver market, in a figurative sense, Silver Reef sank into oblivion as its three major mining operations shut down one by one from 1883 to 1889. By the early 1900s, Silver Reef was a ghost town. But then, a second rush was on when someone involved in tearing down one of the old wood-frame saloons found a leather pouch containing bills and gold coins. When word got out, treasure hunters wrecked most of the other abandoned structures looking for additional hidden caches. Nothing was found, at least that anyone admitted. Only one structure survived intact into the twenty-first century, the old Wells Fargo Express office.

Unlike most ghost towns, which are in remote areas, the community of Leeds has encompassed what used to be Silver Reef. Picturesque remnants of stone walls now stand in the backyards of some of the modern residences in the area. Run by a nonprofit association, the **Silver Reef Museum** (1903 Wells Fargo Rd.; 435-879-2254) is housed in the old Wells Fargo Express office at Leeds. The pre-1879 stone building was added to the National Register of Historical Places in 1971 and restored in the early 1980s. It is considered one of the oldest and best-preserved Wells Fargo offices in the US. Silver Reef's old wooden jail stands across from the museum, and three other Silver Reef structures have been restored along or near what once was a mile-long Main Street.

TOOELE (TOOELE COUNTY)

Primarily a ranching area and timber-harvesting camp settled in the early 1850s by Mormons, Tooele took off with the discovery of silver, gold ore, and copper in the nearby mountains. After that, the town became a smelting center.

The Donner-Reed Party

In the fall of 1846, on the way to California along the Oregon Trail, the Donner-Reed Party got bogged down while crossing the Great Salt Lake desert. Hoping to save their thirsty, overburdened oxen by lightening their loads, the party began jettisoning personal belongings and leaving behind wagons. Many of those items were later discovered and are displayed in the **Donner-Reed Museum** (90 North Cooley St., Grantsville; 435-884-3767). The museum, built from an old pioneer schoolhouse, not only contains Donner-Reed artifacts, but also American Indian cultural material and pioneer relics. The museum is eleven miles northwest of Tooele.

The **Tooele Pioneer Museum** (47 East Vine St.; 435-882-3168) has a wide range of exhibits and artifacts on the history of the Tooele area as well as reference books and other archival materials. One of the museum's highlights is an extensive collection of American Indian artifacts. The **Tooele County Museum** (Vine and Broadway Streets; 435-843-3100) is in the old Tooele Valley Railroad depot, which closed in 1982.

Camp Floyd-Stagecoach Inn State Park

Preparing for an anticipated Mormon rebellion, Washington, DC, sent a large contingent of troops—artillery, infantry, and cavalry plus civilian support personnel—to Utah in 1857. In July 1858, the US Army established Camp Floyd in Cedar Valley south of Salt Lake City. For a time, with 3,500-plus personnel, it was the largest concentration of troops in the nation. War in Utah never materialized, but the garrison, renamed Fort Crittenden in 1860, helped deter Indian depredations and protected the Pony Express and stagecoaches. The post was abandoned in July 1861 following the outbreak of a sure-enough rebellion, the Civil War.

A stagecoach inn built by John Carson remained after the army left, and continued in use until the opening of the transcontinental railroad in 1869. The commissary, only one of several score of buildings once part of the fort, has survived. Listed on the National Register of Historic Places, the former stagecoach stop still stands and is maintained as a state park. The old commissary houses a museum. The **Camp Floyd-Stagecoach Inn State Park** (18035 West 1540 North, Fairfield; 801-768-8932) is thirty miles southeast of Tooele.

VERNAL (UINTAH COUNTY)

Vernal lies in the Uinta Basin of northeastern Utah, an area the Mormons twice rejected for settlement as not suitable for agriculture. The US government set the area aside for Indian use, and it became the home of the Ute and other tribes. Beginning in the late nineteenth century, the government opened the reservation for settlement and Vernal flourished as a cattle town. Its remoteness made it a popular outlaw hangout, Butch Cassidy being the most notable personage known to have spent time in the area. Not long after his release from the Wyoming State Prison in early 1896, the outlaw purchased a new Colt .45 single-action revolver in Vernal, a weapon soon put to good use in Idaho.

Formerly known as the Western Heritage Museum, the **Uintah County Heritage Museum** (155 East Main St.; 435-789-7399) moved into a new, larger building in 2014. The museum has exhibits and informational brochures on American Indians, railroads, mining, and outlaws and the Outlaw Trail. The Salt Lake City–based Daughters of Utah Pioneers also has one of their branch museums in Vernal (186 South 500 West; 435-789-0352).

The Body in the Boat

Plenty of men died at the hands of robbers in the Wild West, and John Jarvie's murder would be no different from the others except for the manner it came to light—twenty-five miles from the scene of the crime, Jarvie's body showed up in an otherwise empty boat snagged in willows along the bank of the Green River in Lodore, Colorado. A Scottish immigrant, Jarvie settled at a well-used crossing of the Green River in 1880 and operated a ferry and general store there. A well-read, educated man and accomplished musician, Jarvie was a popular figure. On July 6, 1909, after forcing Jarvie to open his safe and hand over the money inside, the outlaws shot and killed the sixty-five-year-old storekeeper. Jarvie's sons and lawmen believed they knew who the killers were, but they were never apprehended.

Drive fifty-five miles north from Vernal on US 191, then east twenty-two miles following signs to visit Jarvie Ranch/Browns Park (435-885-3307). Located on federal Bureau of Land Management land, the Jarvie site includes Jarvie's reconstructed residence and general store (which still contains the safe robbed by Jarvie's killers); a two-room dugout where Jarvie and his wife lived during the construction of their residence; a blacksmith shop; and a stone house later built by outlaw Jack Bennett, who learned masonry work while in prison. A final feature is a working replica of the sixteen-foot-diameter waterwheel that Jarvie built. Jarvie is buried in the Ladore, Colorado, cemetery.

Josie Bassett Morris Ranch Complex

She married five times, had a few boyfriends along the way (some say Butch Cassidy was one of them), and twice was tried for cattle theft and acquitted, but no one could question Josie Bassett Morris's grit. Her family came west from Arkansas in 1877 when she was three, homesteading a ranch in the Brown's Park area near the Colorado-Wyoming state line. She married for the first time at nineteen in 1893. Josie and her last husband, Ben Morris, built a cabin in 1913 on land forty miles from her family ranch, where she stayed the rest of her long life (she died at ninety in 1964). Twenty miles east of Vernal off State Highway 149, Josie's homestead and log cabin are now part of Dinosaur National Monument (435-781-7700).

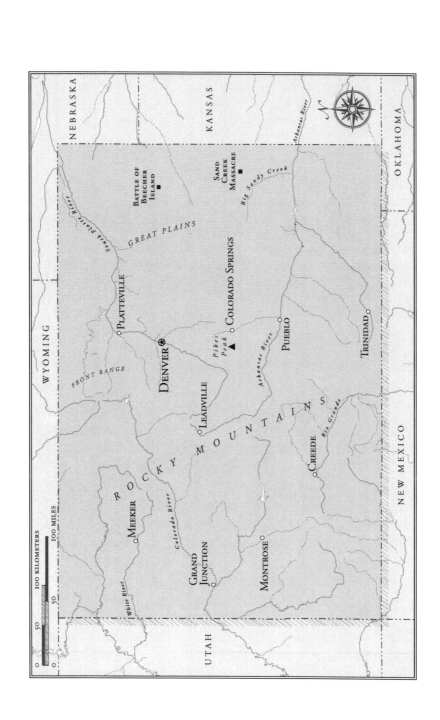

COLORADO

ALAMOSA (ALAMOSA COUNTY)

This town's evocative name comes from the Spanish adjective meaning "of cottonwoods," the word for the cottonwood tree being *álamo*. Founded in 1878 on the Rio Grande in the San Luis Valley as a stop on the newly constructed Denver and Rio Grande Railroad, Alamosa developed as a rail and agricultural center.

The **San Luis Valley Museum** (401 Hunt Ave.; 719-587-0667) focuses on the area's history. Seventeen miles southeast of Alamosa, on the north bank of the Conejos River, is where in 1807 US Army Lt. Zebulon Pike (for whom Pike's Peak was named) first raised the US flag over what was then Spanish territory. Using cottonwood logs, the soldiers constructed a thirty-six-foot-square, twelve-foot-high stockade so they could defend themselves against native peoples if necessary. The men also placed sharpened posts, called pickets, around the fort. And for extra measure, they encircled it with a moat. Indians never attacked, but a troop of Spanish soldiers did show up and took Pike into custody for encroaching on their territory.

In 1926, the State of Colorado purchased 120 acres that included the site and designated it **Pike's Stockade Park.** A decade later, a plaque and monument were placed at the location to commemorate Pike's presence there. A replica of the stockade (22862 County Road 24, Sanford; 719-379-3512) was opened to the public in 1952, and in 1961 the location was named a National Historic Landmark. It is managed by History Colorado, formerly known as the Colorado Historical Society.

Cumbres & Toltec Scenic Railroad

Sooner or later in the history of the Old West, the railroad companies that helped build it reached the end of the line. Most of them went out of business or got acquired by a larger corporation. In many cases, even their trackage disappeared if it was no longer economically useful.

The Cumbres & Toltec Scenic Railroad, dating to 1880 when the Rio Grande Railroad built an extension to serve the silver mining district in the San Juan Mountains of southern Colorado, is a railroad that came back. Now hauling only tourists and railroad buffs, the Cumbres & Toltec operates a vintage steam train from Antonito, Colorado, to Chama, New Mexico, and back.

Revitalized in 1970, the Cumbres & Toltec takes passengers on a scenic, sixty-four-mile trip across open plains, high trestles, and alpine mountain meadows, over 10,015-foot Cumbres Pass, and through two tunnels. Tickets can be purchased at the Antonito Depot (5234 B US 285, Alamosa; 719-472-3984) or online. Antonito is twenty-eight miles south of Alamosa.

ASPEN (PITKIN COUNTY)

Now an internationally known high-country destination, drawing skiers in the winter and fugitives from hotter climes in the summer, Aspen's heritage is thoroughly Old West. Originally known at Ute City, it began in 1879 as a silver mining boomtown. Renamed Aspen in 1880, the town saw its mining peak in the 1890s when for a time it even surpassed Leadville as the nation's top silver-producing district.

Aspen's mining boom attracted New York capitalist Jerome B. Wheeler, who sold his interest in Manhattan's Macy's Department Store and invested heavily in the new Colorado town. In June 1888, construction began on a three-story building that would accommodate a bank Wheeler had founded and the offices of his Aspen Mining and Smelting Co. The top floor housed a large performance venue.

Silver production slowly declined in the early decades of the twentieth century, and by the early 1930s, having once had a population of fifteen thousand, Aspen was approaching ghost town status. However, following World War II, the community reinvented itself as a haven for skiers. But Aspen also has plenty to offer history buffs.

Now known as the **Wheeler Opera House** (320 East Hyman Ave.; 970-920-5770), Wheeler's Romanesque and Italianate–style building still stands and hosts regular entertainment events.

The **Wheeler-Stallard House** (620 West Bleeker St.; 970-925-3721), built by Wheeler for his family in 1888, was later sold to Edgar and Mary Stallard. The Aspen Historical Society purchased it in 1969 and maintains it as a museum. The **Holden-Marolt Mining and Ranching Museum** (40180 State Highway 82; 970-925-3721) interprets the area's industrial and agricultural history.

Built by Wheeler in 1889, the three-story, red-brick **Hotel Jerome** (330 East Main St.; 970-920-1000) managed to survive the mining bust and the Great Depression and continues in operation. Built as a luxury accommodation, it underwent some lean years as a boardinghouse and even stood vacant for a time, but the hotel is once again a luxury property and the social center of the town.

BENT'S FORT (OTERO COUNTY)

Known to grateful travelers as the "Castle on the Plains," the square, adobe-built private fort along the Santa Fe Trail in what is now southeastern Colorado was for a time the largest business enterprise between Kansas City and Santa Fe. For years, it was the only one.

Brothers William and Charles Bent, partnering with Ceran St. Vrain, built the fort in 1833, barely a decade after the Santa Fe Trail had been blazed. As a trading post, it catered to fur trappers and Plains Indians, particularly the Southern Cheyenne and Arapaho. The partners' business grew, with satellite fortified posts to the north and south and company stores in Taos and Santa Fe.

Bent's Fort was a heavily fortified oasis where travelers could get water, food, and supplies. Farriers and wheelwrights at the fort shod horses and repaired wagons. Legendary scout Kit Carson worked as a hunter for the Bent brothers in 1841 and spent time at the fort, as did explorer John C. Fremont. When the war with Mexico began in 1846, Col. Stephen Watts Kearny's "Army of the West" staged there before invading New Mexico.

After sixteen years as a waypoint on the plains, the fort was abandoned in 1849 and slowly deteriorated. The location was designated as a National Historic Site in 1960, but more than a decade and a half passed before the National Park Service—relying on descriptive nineteenth-century documents backed up by archaeological work—reconstructed the old trading post (35110 State Highway 194 East, La Junta; 719-383-5010) at its original location. Opened during the 1976 US Bicentennial, **Bent's Fort** is one of the Old West's more significant historic sites. The **Otero Museum** (706 West 3rd St., La Junta; 719-384-7500) focuses on the county's history. The museum complex includes four modern buildings and three restored historic structures.

BOULDER (BOULDER COUNTY)

Appropriately named for a town in the Rocky Mountains, Boulder was settled as a mining supply town in the 1860s. Boulder has two historic districts: its downtown with numerous nineteenth- and early twentieth-century buildings of varying architectural styles, and the Mapleton Hill District, a turn-of-the-twentieth-century residential area. A self-guided tour of both areas is available at **Historic Boulder** (646 Pearl St.) and at the **Museum of Boulder** (2205 Broadway; 303-449-3464).

Thomas Horn Jr.

Ex-army scout, cowboy, range detective, Pinkerton operative, and hired gun Tom Horn worked out of the Denver office of the national Pinkerton Detective Agency from 1889 to 1890. One of Horn's more notable Colorado cases involved tracking train robbers Thomas Eskridge (aka "Peg-Leg" Watson) and Burt Curtis—from Fremont County, Colorado, to the Washita River in Indian Territory (Oklahoma) in the summer of 1890—and bringing them in peacefully. When Horn got involved in the bloody Johnson County War in Wyoming, it proved his undoing, and he was hanged for murder in Cheyenne in 1903. His older brother

Charles lived in Boulder and had Horn's remains shipped here for burial. For several weeks after the funeral, the family paid to have armed guards watch their already famous relative's grave for fear someone would steal his body and put it on exhibition. Horn (1860–1903) is buried in **Columbia Cemetery** (1201 9th St.; section C, lot 74, space 4). Next to his grave is the final resting place of his brother, who joined him in death in 1930.

BROWN'S PARK (MOFFAT COUNTY)

Brown's Park had "Park" in its name long before it became the undeveloped equivalent of one when the federal government made much of the Green River Valley a national wildlife refuge in 1965. Well before then, as a favorite cooling-off place for outlaws like Butch Cassidy, it had seen plenty of wildlife of a different sort.

Other than the rugged, isolated landscape that made it such an attractive hideout for bad men, in the late nineteenth century and well into the twentieth century, two sisters named Ann and Josie Bassett—whose parents ranched in Brown's Park—added to the scenery and the lore. Some have said Cassidy was sweet on both. While that has never been proven, there's no doubt they knew each other.

Josie was the oldest and lived the longest, never leaving the park though she eventually got scammed out of the land she inherited. Her little sister Ann left after being acquitted of cattle rustling. She married in 1923 and moved with her husband to Utah. Josie also married—five times.

Following her death at ninety after falling from a horse, Josie was buried in the Bassett family cemetery on private property a half mile north of County Road 318 (GPS coordinates: N40° 46.66', W108° 50.79'). Ann's ashes, as had been her wish, were scattered on what had been her family's land, but only after her husband died six years later. In the interim, he had kept her remains in the trunk of his car.

BUENA VISTA (CHAFFEE COUNTY)

Some of the earliest placer gold mining in the territory took place along the upper Arkansas River in central Colorado's high country. By 1861, a mining camp called Granite had developed where Cache Creek emptied into the river, its population quickly swelling to three thousand. The same year, the territorial legislature created the future state's first seventeen political subdivisions, one of them Lake County. The first county seat was Dayton, a town not far from Granite, but in 1868 Granite became the new Lake County capital.

A Decidedly Dangerous Committee of Safety

What came to be called the **Lake County War** had nothing to do with subduing hostile American Indians or political differences. Essentially, it was a violent conflict between two factions—vigilantes calling themselves a "Committee of Safety" versus a clandestine group of suspected claim jumpers and assorted scoundrels known as "Regulators." Not that the county did not have law enforcement and a judiciary, but government officials, some clearly partisan to one side or the other, proved unable to contain a series of violent events that climaxed on July 3, 1875, with the murder of Judge Elias Dyer in his own courtroom at Granite.

Though the assassination occurred while the Committee of Safety had the courthouse surrounded, Dyer's killer was never apprehended. Following a quiet threat from the governor to send in troops (he did not want to unfavorably impact Colorado's chances for statehood), passions waned, and no further violence occurred. Four years later, the legislature cut a chunk of land from Lake County to create Chaffee County. That 1879 redrawing of lines on the map soon brought more trouble.

The Courthouse Raid

Seventeen miles southeast of Granite lay an agricultural community called Buena Vista. With the discovery of silver around Leadville, Buena Vista became a waypoint on the main route to the mines and soon gained a railroad connection. Following the creation of the new county, the matter of where the county seat should be was put to the electorate. Voters chose Buena Vista over Granite.

Even though the Lake County War had fizzled, many of its veterans were still around, and they had already demonstrated a willingness to ignore the rule of law. Accordingly, the powers that be in Granite vowed that they would not give up their courthouse. In response, a delegation of Buena Vista citizens commandeered a locomotive and flatcar and headed to Granite to forcibly claim the county records and move them to the lawful county seat.

Late at night on November 12, 1880, the Buena Vista men held Sheriff John Mear at gunpoint as they emptied the courthouse. Not only did the pro–Buena Vista faction load county records onto the train, but the men requisitioned the furniture and even the courtroom railing. Of course, Buena Vista did not yet have a courthouse, so the records were placed in the safes of several local businesses. Realizing they had no legal standing in the matter, the citizenry of Granite did not further contest the loss of their county seat status.

The cornerstone for a new two-story brick courthouse was laid June 8, 1882, with construction continuing for the next two years. It shouldn't have taken that long to build the new courthouse, but cost overruns and other issues delayed things. Buena Vista enjoyed its county seat status for forty-eight years, but Granite—by then the next closest thing to a ghost town—got the last laugh in 1928 when voters decided to move the county government to Salinda.

After the seat of Chaffee County moved to Salinda, the 1882 courthouse at 506 East Main Street in Buena Vista was used as a school until 1972. The school district sold the building to the town government, which turned it over to the local historical society for use as a museum. Judge Dyer was buried in Granite Cemetery, but in 1878 his family had his remains removed from the town where he had been murdered and reburied in **Cedar Hill Cemetery** (800 East Wolfensberger Rd., Castle Rock; GPS coordinates: N39° 22.79', W104° 52.35'). His gravestone notes, "A victim of the murderous mob ruling in Lake County."

CAÑON CITY (FREMONT COUNTY)

Founded in 1860 during the second year of the Pike's Peak gold rush, Cañon City picked up momentum a decade later when it became home of the Colorado Territorial Prison. Later, the arrival of the Santa Fe Railroad enlivened things even more, though given the presence of the prison, the town was a reasonably peaceful place to live—at least for those outside the walls. The Cañon City Historic District includes eighty historic structures.

Built in 1871 when Colorado was still a territory, the old territorial prison known as "Old Max" has been in use ever since. Historic as it is, it is not open to public tours, but visitors can learn all about it and prison culture in general at the adjacent **Museum of Colorado Prisons** (201 North 1st St.; 719-269-3015). Located in the former Women's Prison, built in 1935 and closed in 1968, the museum opened in 1988. Exhibits cover the full range of the old prison's history, including one of its more famous "guests," convicted Donner-Reed Party cannibal Alfred Packer.

A Traveling Hotel

Most Old West hotels catered to travelers who came by rail, but the **St. Cloud Hotel** itself arrived in Cañon City by train. First built in Silver Cliff, Colorado, during its short-lived silver mining boom, when the ore played out so did the St. Cloud. Accordingly, the proprietor had the hostelry carefully taken apart and shipped in pieces in freight wagons to Westcliff, where the hotel was loaded onto Denver and Rio Grande Railroad flatcars and taken to Cañon City. Rebuilt as soon as possible, the hotel reigned for generations as the city's premier place to stay. Buffalo Bill and Calamity Jane stayed there, and from 1910 to 1913 the St. Cloud accommodated the offices of Selig Polyscope, a company that produced silent movies, which brought in early-day Western stars like Tom Mix. The hotel (627-631 Main St., St. Cloud) has had a variety of owners and names, but in recent years has stood vacant.

CENTRAL CITY (GILPEN COUNTY)

A decade after the discovery of gold transformed California in the late 1840s and early 1850s, John H. Gregory found a rich lode of placer gold in a ravine in what is now Colorado's Gilpen County and staked a claim. The geologic feature became known as Gregory Gulch. Other veins were found in the vicinity, and by 1860, ten thousand people had descended on the area hoping to get rich. A miner's camp first called Gregory's Diggings and then Mountain City soon evolved into the boomtown of Central City.

The easy pickings played out in a few years, but after the Civil War a second boom came when a smelter built at the nearby town of Black Hawk made it feasible to mine gold ore. Black Hawk developed as a working man's town, while Central City became "the grand lady of the Rockies." Also touted as the "richest square mile on earth," for a time it rivaled Denver (only thirty-seven miles away) in importance. It boasted a luxury hotel, a fine opera house, and other trappings of a refined community.

Mining in the area continued into the 1930s, but Central City reached its peak population in 1900. Each decade from the 1880s on, gold ore production steadily declined as both Central City and Black Hawk slid toward ghost town status. State legislation allowing for casino gambling perked up both towns in the 1990s, but more so for Black Hawk than Central City.

Many gold rush–era buildings in downtown Central City and the Black Hawk Historic District still stand, though Central City is the best preserved. Among the more notable structures there are the 1872 **Teller House** (120 Eureka St.), once an upscale, four-story brick hotel whose guests included President Ulysses S. Grant; the 750-seat 1878 **Opera House** (124 Eureka St.; 303-292-6700); and the 1867 **Thomas Billings house** (209 Eureka St.; 303-582-5848). Located in the 1869 Central City schoolhouse, the **Gilpin Historical Museum** (228 East First High St.; 303-582-5283) tell the story of the area.

CHIVINGTON (KIOWA COUNTY)

Established in 2007, the **Sand Creek Massacre National Historic Site** (55411 County Road West; 719-438-5916) is located eight miles north of Chivington. The site can be reached via State Highway 96, turning north onto Chief White Antelope Way (County Road 54) or County Road 59. The remote site, previously marked only by a red granite monument labeled "Sand Creek Battle Ground/Nov. 29 & 30, 1864" has interpretive signage and a visitor center with exhibits explaining the battle.

The Sand Creek Massacre

What transpired at a still-desolate bend of Sand Creek in southeastern Colorado on November 29, 1864, changed the history of the Great Plains. Before that day, despite years of intermittent hostile acts on the part of both whites and Plains Indians, at least some Indian chiefs held to the hope of peaceful relations with Euro-Americans even as more and more settlers encroached on their land. But then came the events of that cold, late fall day.

Forced to new winter campgrounds by a scarcity of buffalo and firewood in their traditional campsites, in the fall of 1864, Black Kettle, White Antelope, and Left Hand led their people to a bend in Sand Creek in what is now Kiowa County. More than a hundred tepees stood in the valley, with hundreds of horses grazing nearby. Though Black Kettle had been assured of protection by regular federal troops stationed at Fort Lyon, Colorado (even though they had been told they couldn't camp near the post), two regiments of Colorado militiamen led by Col. John M. Chivington viewed the 750 or so American Indians on Sand Creek—mostly Cheyennes but some Arapahos—as hostiles who posed a threat to their territory.

On the morning of November 29, the roughly seven hundred Colorado volunteers attacked the encampment, even though Black Kettle was flying a US flag over his lodge to demonstrate his peaceful intentions. Artillery fire raked the camp, followed by a mounted charge that left two hundred to three hundred Indians dead, half of them women and children. Though many whites, including some of the volunteers, were sickened by the senseless massacre, neither Chivington nor any of his officers suffered any consequences for their actions. But the attitude of most Plains Indians toward the whites had been changed forever, for the worse. There would be more massacres of Indians and whites as the clash of cultures continued in the West for more than thirty years.

Colorado Springs (El Paso County)

With the Pike's Peak gold rush well under way, in the spring of 1859 a group of investors platted a two-square-mile townsite just east of the Rocky Mountains in what is now El Paso County. They named it Colorado City for the extensive outcroppings of red rock in the vicinity, *colorado* being Spanish for "red." Initially, the new town lay on the far western edge of Kansas Territory, but that fall it became part of locally organized Jefferson Territory, an entity the US government never recognized. So Colorado City technically remained part of Kansas until Congress approved the creation of Colorado Territory in 1861. Colorado City became its capital—but less than a week later, territorial legislators voted to move the new territorial government to Denver.

The town did not pan out as the commercial and transportation center its founders had expected, but for a time it did do quite well as a place where miners could spend their money on booze, opium, women, or games of chance. Meanwhile, the more recently founded nearby town of Colorado Springs took a higher road and banned alcohol. Whether it was clean living or for other reasons, Colorado Springs began to grow while Colorado City did not. In 1917, the former annexed the latter.

Though Colorado City did not survive as a separate community, many of its gold rush–era structures still stand, despite two fires, and are included in the historic district listed on the National Register of Historic Places. In the Thomas MacLaren–designed 1903 El Paso County Courthouse, the **Colorado Springs Pioneers Museum** (215 South Tejon St.; 719-385-5990) has exhibits on the history of old Colorado City, Colorado Springs, and the Pike's Peak region. Colorado Springs has two other museums, the **Ghost Town Museum** (400 South 21st St.; 719-634-0696) and the **Western Museum of Mining and Industry** (225 North Gate Blvd.; 719-488-0880).

CRAIG (MOFFAT COUNTY)

Though some settlers had been in the area since the early 1880s, the town of Craig came later when William H. Tucker arrived from Glenwood Springs to lay out a townsite in anticipation of the coming Denver Northwestern and Pacific Railroad. He named the town in honor of the investor who had fronted the most money, the Rev. William Bayard Craig. A ranching center, the town was incorporated in 1908.

Wild Bunch Photo Op

In 1898, lawmen recaptured Wild Bunch outlaw Harry Tracy in Brown's Park after he escaped prison and murdered posse member Valentine Hoy. Tracy and fellow bad man David Lant were taken to the Routt County jail at Hahn's Peak. En route, the lawmen and their prisoners spent the night at the Royal Hotel in Craig. There the officers allowed photographers Amos Bennett and D.W. Diamond to photograph the dangerous duo. But their work, while constituting the only known non-mugshot or non-death image of either man, was not perfect. The photo of Tracy (held by the Tread of Pioneers Museum in Steamboat Springs, Colorado) does not show his shackled legs, and the image of Lant (held by the Museum of Northwest Colorado in Craig) shows his legs but is fuzzy. Using photo-editing technology, the Museum of Northwest Colorado combined the best of both photos for a striking collage of Tracy. The staff member doing the work then added a bit of color to the image, in a digital way bringing the outlaw back to life for museum visitors.

Founded as the Moffat County Museum in 1964, since 1991 the **Museum of Northwest Colorado** (590 Yampa Ave.; 970-824-6360) has occupied the old state armory. The museum's exhibits are heavy on cowboy gear, firearms, railroad history, and the Butch Cassidy gang, including the newly enhanced image of Harry Tracy.

CREEDE (MINERAL COUNTY)

In 1889, a prospector named Nicholas Creede found a rich out-cropping of silver ore in what later became Mineral County. "Holy Moses!" he supposedly proclaimed. When he filed his claim, Holy Moses seemed like an appropriate name. Mining began in earnest in 1890, and the camp that became yet another Colorado boomtown, for a time called Jimtown, took the name of the man who discovered the lode.

Soapy Smith Bubbles Up and Robert Ford Gets His

When it became expedient to vacate Denver during one of that city's periodic social reform movements, con man **Soapy Smith** and his associates moved their operations to Creede. In February

1892, Smith opened the Orleans Club on Main Street (also known as Creede Avenue) as a gambling and drinking venue. Beginning in April, he supplemented his income with an innovative scam. Announcing that he had purchased a petrified man found by a miner, Smith put the body—he called him McGinty—on display for a dime a look. While those who fell for the hoax waited in line to see the "amazing" discovery, Smith and his associates took them for more money in games of three-card monte. His principal business rival was a man named Robert Ford who, along with his mistress, ran a casino, saloon, and bawdy house called Ford's Exchange. Smith did not like anyone else getting some of his action, but as it turned out, neither he nor Ford would be around much longer. After circumstances changed in his favor in Denver, Smith returned to the larger city and took McGinty with him.

Smith left just in time. Fire destroyed virtually the entire town of Creede on June 5, 1892. Not wanting his cash flow interrupted, Ford quickly reopened his bar in a tent, but he would not be staying in business for long. Four days later, a drifter named Edward Kelley entered his establishment and gave Ford a fatally deep haircut with a scattergun. Why Kelley killed Ford has long been a matter of speculation. Most figured it was for the notoriety of it. After all, Robert Ford—better known as Bob—was the "dirty little coward" who had killed Jesse James a decade before.

Housed in the old Denver and Rio Grande Railroad depot, the **Creede Historical Museum and Library** (15 Main St.; 719-658-2004) tells the story of this historic mining town. The wood-frame depot was built in 1891–1892 when the Denver and Rio Grande extended its narrow-gauge line to Creede to accommodate mining operations and the town's sudden population of ten thousand. The line is said to have paid for itself in only four months. Items on display at the museum include Creede's first fire wagon, a hand-drawn contraption; a horse-drawn hearse; gambling paraphernalia; and other artifacts. The old depot also holds the archives of the Creede Historical Society.

Rusty wrought-iron and weathered wood fences surround the graves of Creede pioneers in **Old Creede Cemetery** (half a mile south of town off County Road 504 on Bee McClure Drive). Robert Ford was initially buried here, but his remains were later exhumed and sent to Richmond, Missouri, for reburial. For the sake of tourists, there's a marker where his grave used to be.

CRESTED BUTTE (GUNNISON COUNTY)

Crested Butte began as a supply point for silver miners in the 1870s. Howard Smith laid out the town in 1878 and opened a smelter and sawmill, but the arrival of the Denver and Rio Grande Railroad stimulated a demand for coal, and plenty of it had been found around Crested Butte. The silver panic of 1893 did away with the area's silver mines, and from then until 1952 Crested Butte was a coal mining town. After that, the town's biggest natural resource changed from black to white—as in the ample annual snowfall that enabled its development as a ski resort.

Many of the town's old buildings still stand. A self-guided walking tour of the downtown historic district is available from the **Crested Butte Chamber of Commerce** (904 South Main St.; 719-658-2374) or the **Crested Butte Mountain Heritage Museum** (331 Elk Ave.; 970-349-1880).

Captain Jack

Originally from Nottingham, England, Captain Jack arrived in Gunnison County in 1880 hoping to stake a silver claim. Hundreds of prospectors around Crested Butte had the same notion, but there was one big difference: Captain Jack was a woman. Her legal name was Ellen E. Jack, but after losing two of her three children to disease, soon followed by the death of her husband—former naval officer Captain Charles Jack—she decided to take his name. She also headed West, diamonds and negotiable government bonds sewn into her skirt.

Unlike so many Western women forced to support themselves when widowed or deserted, Captain Jack did not resort to prostitution. She ran boardinghouses and invested in the Black Queen Mine, and though seen as eccentric, she became a respected resident. She also became a writer, setting down an action-filled life story in an autobiography that surely had some truth to it. She left the Crested Butte area in 1900 and spent the rest of her life in Colorado Springs. She died there in 1921, just shy of eighty.

Ellen Elliott Jack (1842–1921) is buried in **Evergreen Cemetery** (1005 South Hancock Ave., Colorado Springs; block 00074 000005-0000NW; GPS coordinates: N38° 49.03', W104° 47.93').

CRIPPLE CREEK (TELLER COUNTY)

By 1890, conventional wisdom held that all the significant gold deposits in Colorado had been found. The Cripple Creek area was ranching country with fewer than five hundred residents. A cowboy named Bob Womack had found traces of placer gold in 1878 in the vicinity, and while he had a notion that the area held more than traces of the precious metal, it wasn't until the fall of 1890 that he got around to staking a claim. Womack continued to believe he was on to something, but no one else did—at least not until the spring of 1891, when self-taught mineralogist Ed De LaVergne came from Colorado Springs to look at Womack's ore samples. He had seen gold ore in Europe and was convinced that Womack had indeed found the real thing. He believed it so much he staked his own claim in April 1891, the beginning of the Cripple Creek Mining District. By summer, another American gold boom was on.

At the height of the frenzy, Cripple Creek and other mining camps around it supported some 150 saloons, along with dance halls, theaters, hotels, restaurants, shops, and a large red-light district. There were fourteen competing newspapers, forty-one assay offices, forty-six brokerage houses, and ninety-one lawyers. Nearly five hundred mines extracted millions in gold each year. With more than twenty-five thousand people in the area—some claimed fifty thousand—Cripple Creek saw its peak production in 1901. Although the major mines remained active until after World War II, the last one did not close until 1962.

Despite two devastating fires in 1896, many of the city's historic structures still stand, and since the state's legalization of limited-stakes gambling in 1991, Cripple Creek is a popular tourist destination. And gold mining, this time from an open pit at the site of the former Cresson Mine, resumed in the mid-1990s. More gold (over twenty-two million ounces) has come out of the Cripple Creek Mining District than in California and Alaska combined.

A Case of Legal Skullduggery

Bartender William Brooks surely intended only to curb miner James Roberts's drunken exuberance when he cracked him on the head with the butt of his .45. As would be expected, Roberts crumpled to the barroom floor. As would not be expected, the blow he sustained that Christmas night of 1901 killed him. Arrested for Roberts's murder, Brooks retained well-regarded attorney J. Maurice Finn.

Finn knew that many an unruly cowboy over the years had been "buffaloed" (knocked out by a blow from a pistol) and wondered why in Roberts's case it had been fatal. With a bit of skullduggery and the cooperation of a local doctor, Finn found that the victim had been born with an abnormally thin skull. Cleverly getting the sawed-off top of Roberts's skull admitted to evidence, Finn won acquittal for his client. Brooks may have been found innocent, but Roberts's fellow miners didn't see it that way. The barkeep barely made it out of town ahead of a lynch mob.

Roberts was buried in Mount Pishta Cemetery—all but the top of his skull, that is. For more than a century, his crushed cranium lay in the evidence room at the courthouse. A newspaper reporter learned about it in 2010 and convinced the district attorney to donate the skull to the Cripple Creek District

Museum. (The skull can't be buried with the rest of Roberts because his grave site has been lost.) Located since 1953 in the 1895 Midland Terminal Railroad depot, the **Cripple Creek District Museum** (510 Bennett Dr.; 719-689-9540) has exhibits focusing on the community's mining and railroad history.

Occupying the red-brick building that served as the Teller County jail for nearly ninety years—the original cells are still in place—the **Cripple Creek Outlaws and Lawmen Jail Museum** (136 West Bennett Ave.; 719-689-6556) gives visitors a feel for the shadier side of life in a gold mining boomtown and the peace officers who endeavored to keep it relatively civilized. In addition to all the lesser-known miscreants and felons who at one time or another cooled their heels here, the lockup once accommodated Robert Curry (aka Bob Lee), a member of the Wild Bunch gang. Displays include copies of early city ordinances, 1890s-vintage police logs, and newspaper accounts of local crimes.

The establishment known as the **Old Homestead House** (353 Myers Ave.; 719-689-9090) had a name evocative of domestic tranquility and marital fidelity, but it was an upscale brothel run by Pearl DeVere. She and her high-class ladies catered to the boomtown's wealthier gentlemen. Built in 1896 and opened as a museum in 1958, the Old Homestead House is Cripple Creek's last standing former bordello and one of only a handful in the West.

Opened in 1891, the **Mollie Kathleen Mine** (9388 State Highway 67; 719-689-2466) has been conducting tours more than seventy years. The tour begins with a one-thousand-foot vertical decent down the gold mine's shaft. A hundred stories beneath the earth's surface, visitors learn about the history of underground mining from the 1890s to modern times. Not only will visitors see gold veins, they'll get a free gold ore sample.

DELTA (DELTA COUNTY)

A Six-Shooter Withdrawal

With the nation mired in the worst financial depression to that point in its history, Bill McCarty and his son Fred walked into Delta's Farmers and Merchants Bank on the morning of September 7, 1893, to make a "withdrawal." Bill's brother Tom stood in the alley behind the bank holding their horses. Bank co-founder and cashier Andrew T. Blanchly handed the robbers roughly $700 in cash and change, but then, thinking Blanchly might be going for a gun, young Fred panicked and fatally shot the hapless bank employee in the neck. Hearing the gunfire from across the street, hardware store owner W. Ray Simpson grabbed his .50-caliber Sharps rifle and ran outside in time to see Bill, Fred, and Tom galloping away from the bank. From 240 feet away, Simpson took aim and put a bullet in Bill's head. Then, now from a full block away, he dropped Fred. The robbery turned out to be a windfall for a local photographer, who made good money selling images of the propped-up dead outlaws for twenty-five cents each. Tom McCarty escaped and lived in Washington State until at least 1917. Researchers have not determined what became of him after that.

The surviving children of the slain bank teller placed a marker at the site of the bank, 316 Main Street, in 1958. Blanchly was buried in **Delta Cemetery** (1055 East 3rd St., block 1, lot 11). The two outlaws were buried in an unmarked grave—reportedly in the same pine box. In 2001, a marker was placed at block 2, lot 180, space 4, in the approximate location of their grave. The rifle used to kill the two robbers, and the pistols they carried, are displayed at the **Delta County Historical Museum** (251 Meeker St.; 970-874-8721).

DENVER (DENVER COUNTY)

The gilded dome atop Colorado's capitol is one of the most appropriate pieces of ornamentation in the West given that Denver, and Colorado, both owe their birth to gold. But no monuments honor the man who found it, John Beck.

A Cherokee on his way to the California goldfields, Beck stopped in 1850 to pan for gold in Ralston Creek, a stream on the plains just east of the Rockies at a place that would come to be called Denver. He found gold dust but did not think it amounted to much. However, nine years later, with a party of other prospectors, he returned to the area. This time they discovered a significant amount of placer gold in Cherry Creek. Soon the nation's second great gold boom was on, and by 1860 Denver was well on its way to becoming one of the West's most important cities.

The four-story **Colorado History Center** (1200 North Broadway; 303-447-8679) includes permanent and rotating exhibits on the history of Denver and the state. The greater Denver area has many other museums with a wide range of focus.

Slave to Entrepreneur

Born a slave in Virginia in 1822, as a teenager Barney Lancelot Ford escaped his servitude via the Underground Railroad. After reaching Chicago, he taught himself to read and write and became a barber. As a slave, he did not have a last name, but when he married Julia Lyon in Chicago, she suggested he take a middle and last name from a steam engine—the Lancelot Ford. In 1860, still a fugitive slave, Ford traveled from Illinois to Colorado to seek his fortune in the newly discovered goldfields. His wife soon joined him there.

The couple settled in Breckenridge, where Ford staked a claim but got cheated out of it. Undaunted, he opened a barbershop in nearby Denver. When fire destroyed it, he used his earnings to leverage a loan that enabled him to build a new barbershop along with a restaurant and hotel. In turn, the income from those properties enabled him to build a lavish four-story hotel, the Inter Ocean, at 16th and Blake Streets. In addition to managing the business enterprises that made him wealthy, Ford was a pioneer civil rights activist.

The Inter Ocean Hotel was eventually razed, but the three-story building that housed his restaurant still stands at 1514 Blake Street. His former residence (111 East Washington Ave., Breckenridge; 970-453-9767) is now the **Barney Ford House Museum.** Barney Ford Hill in Breckenridge was named in his honor, as was a public school in Denver. A stained-glass portrait of Ford hangs in the state capitol.

The Man Who Founded the *Rocky*

For nearly 150 years the feisty *Rocky Mountain News* (informally known as "the Rocky") both chronicled and made Denver history. The newspaper was founded in 1859 by William Newton Byers, not long after he came West seeking gold. In 1883, by then a successful businessman and tireless booster of Denver as the "Queen City of the West," Byers built a two-story brick house for his family and lived there for six years before selling it. The buyer was William Evans, son of Colorado's second territorial governor. Now known as the **Byers-Evans House**, the two-story brick structure is owned by the Colorado Historical Society and hosts a museum (1310 Bannock St.; 303-620-4933). The historical society offers guided tours of the old house. Byers (1831–1903) is buried in Fairmount Cemetery.

The **Buckhorn Exchange** (1000 Osage St.; 303-534-9505) is one of Denver's oldest surviving buildings and one of the West's longest-running eateries. Built in 1888 by Neef Brothers Brewing Co., the stone building was acquired in 1893 by Henry H. "Shorty Scout" Zietz, a friend of Buffalo Bill Cody. He first ran it as a saloon called the Rio Grande Exchange, but later began serving meals and changed the name to Buckhorn Exchange. Cattlemen, railroad men, miners, gamblers, and businessmen frequented the establishment, its walls decorated with trophy game mounts. "Shorty" had a lot of friends, including President Theodore Roosevelt and numerous American Indians. It is still a restaurant and is known as Denver's original steakhouse.

Built in 1892 of sandstone and granite, the four-hundred-room **Brown Palace** (321 17th St.; 303-297-3111) became one of the West's best-known hotels. Named for its first owner, pioneer Denver resident and real estate investor Henry C. Brown, the hotel has hosted the famous and the infamous over the years. (Now a luxury property, the number of rooms has been reduced to 241.) Designed by noted architect Frank Edbrooke, the nine-story hotel took nearly four years to build and, counting its furnishings, cost $2 million—then a staggering amount of money.

The House of Lions

Before April 15, 1912, Margaret Tobin Brown was only a rich miner's wife generally snubbed by snooty Denver society women. But that changed after she saved a lifeboat full of passengers who had managed to make it off the sinking luxury liner *Titanic* after it struck an iceberg in the Atlantic. From then on, she was known as the "Unsinkable Molly Brown." She came to Denver from Leadville, Colorado, with her husband James J. Brown, who had made a fortune off the silver mine known as the Little Jonny. In 1894 Brown purchased a cut-stone, Queen Ann–style mansion noted for the two carved lions guarding its entrance. Following her death in 1932, the mansion became a home for wayward girls and saw several other uses. By 1970 it faced demolition before Historic Denver, Inc. bought it and turned it into a museum. The **Molly Brown House Museum** (1340 Pennsylvania St.; 303-832-4092) has been restored to its 1910 appearance.

The Day the Wild West Died

On January 10, 1917, William F. Cody, far better known simply as Buffalo Bill, died at his sister May's house in Denver. The Wild West that Cody had known was already long gone, but his death made that fact so much more obvious. Five days later, his body lay in state beneath the grand staircase in the rotunda of the Colorado capitol. Some twenty-five thousand people filed by his open casket and thousands more got turned away. Following the public viewing, the old showman's casket was placed in storage at a Denver funeral home until he could be buried, as he had requested, on Lookout Mountain near Golden, Colorado. From there, he had told his family, he could see four western states. The Queen Ann–style two-story house where Cody died still stands at 2932 Lafayette Street. It has been restored and is privately owned and not open to the public. The 1894 state capitol where he lay in state is at 200 East Colfax Avenue, Denver.

Well-known Denver crime boss "Big Ed" Chase and con man Soapy Smith opened the **Tivoli Club** in 1888. The club had a downstairs saloon and upstairs gambling, with faro, roulette tables, and a poker room. Legend has it that Smith, clearly a man with a sense of humor, placed a sign at the bottom of the stairs reading "Caveat Emptor." Most visitors lost their money in the rigged games, and some more than that. The *Rocky Mountain News* referred to the Tivoli as "the slaughter pen" and vigorously crusaded against Smith and his pals. In 1890 the name was changed to the Silver Club, but after a while the place was again called the Tivoli. The club occupied a two-story building at 1337-1339 17th Street, on the southeast corner at Market Street in Denver. A high-rise bank covers the site today.

Tom Horn's Boss

While working out of the Denver Pinkerton office, Tom Horn reported to Pinkerton superintendent James McParland. McParland was a veteran Irish-born operative who had made his reputation in the mid-1870s breaking up the Molly McGuires in Pennsylvania and with his notable casework in the West. By 1903, still based in Denver, McParland had risen to Western Division manager. The Pinkerton headquarters stood at 16th and Arapahoe. McParland lived with his family at 1256 Columbine Street in a house that still stands. He died on May 18, 1919, in Denver and is buried in **Mount Olivet Cemetery** (12801 West 44th Ave., Wheat Ridge; 303-424-7785).

Founded in 1876, **Riverside Cemetery** (5201 Brighton Blvd.; 303-399-0692) is Denver's oldest cemetery. Among numerous notables buried there is **Augusta Louise Pierce Tabor** (1833–1895); Colorado lawman and private detective agency founder **David J. Cook** (1840–1907); and **Barney Ford** (1822–1902).

Denver's second-oldest cemetery, **Fairmount Cemetery** (430 South Quebec St.; 303-399-0692) was founded in 1890. At the time, its 280 acres amounted to the largest developed landscape west of the Mississippi. Noted Colorado landscape architect Reinhard Schuetze planned the cemetery, which includes two historic landmarks, the Little Ivy Chapel and the Gate Lodge. Graves in the cemetery constitute a Who's Who of Colorado history. Among the notable Old West figures buried here are **Lou Blonger** (1849–1924), saloonkeeper, gambling house owner, and Denver underworld kingpin; **John Milton Chivington** (1821–1894), Methodist pastor, Union army colonel, and ranking officer in the Sand Creek Massacre; **John Wesley Iliff** (1831–1878), known as the Cattle King of the Plains; and Western writer **William MacLeod Raine** (1871–1954).

Denver's best-known madam, **Mattie Silks,** is also buried in Fairmount Cemetery. The famous brothel owner seldom lacked for company in life, and even in death Mattie Silks still receives visitors. But no one will find her grave looking for a headstone with that name. Nor, despite all the money she made, does she lie beneath an imposing grave marker. All it says is, "Martha A. Ready, Died January 7, 1929" (block 12, lot 131, northeast section).

Next to her, in an unmarked grave, is her first husband. (Census records show his last name variously as Thomson or Thompson, his first name varying from Cortege to Cortez. All sources agree that he went by Cort.) Mattie's second husband, Jack Ready, is also buried in Fairmount, in an unmarked grave in block 51.

Mattie Silks

Before opening a pleasure palace in Denver in 1876, Mattie operated a Dodge City brothel. When that Kansas town's trail-herding days ended, so did her cash flow. In fast-growing Denver, Mattie's only concern was competition. To the delight of newspaper editors, she feuded verbally and occasionally physically with rival madams, including Jennie Rogers and Kate Fulton.

In 1881 rivalry between Mattie and Kate led to a Wild West rarity, two women shooting it out. On this occasion, however, the fight was over the affections of gambler and con man Cort Thomson. Though the ladies faced each other only feet apart, Kate missed Mattie and Mattie missed Kate. But Thomson, who until that point had been watching with amusement as the two women argued over him, caught one of Mattie's stray bullets. Thomson recovered, and three years later, he and Mattie married, the beginning of a stormy, off-and-on relationship—though they never divorced.

The Klondike gold rush attracted Mattie and Thomson to Skagway, Alaska, in 1898, but she didn't like the weather and the couple soon returned to Denver. Since their marriage, Thomson had been living off Mattie's money. Two years younger than her, he died at fifty-two in 1900, likely from years of alcohol and opium abuse. Mattie paid for his funeral, but for whatever reason never got around to putting up a tombstone for him.

Denver cleaned up its act in 1915 and open prostitution ended. By then Mattie owned a ranch near Wray, Colorado, had real estate investments, and made and lost money playing the ponies at Overland Park. She had married again, this time to her former bouncer, John Dillon "Handsome Jack" Ready.

No one knows why, but after she died at eighty-three from complications of a fall in 1929, she was laid to rest next to her first husband. When husband No. 2 died two years after Mattie, he was buried in the same cemetery, but not near Mattie.

Mattie's best-known business, The House of Mirrors, stood at 1942 Market Street. The gunfight with Fulton took place on the west bank of the South Platte River near the present Larimer Street viaduct. At the time of her death, her address was 2835 Lawrence Street.

Durango (La Plata County)

From the laying of its first tracks in 1870, the Denver and Rio Grande Railroad eventually connected Colorado, Utah, and New Mexico. When widespread silver mining began in Colorado's San Juan Mountains, the railroad extended a narrow-gauge line northward to booming Silverton. The line originated at Durango, which the railroad founded in 1880, and connected with Silverton in 1882. The D&RG eventually was absorbed by what is now the Union Pacific Railroad, but the scenic narrow-gauge route from Durango to Silverton (now the Durango and Silverton Railroad) remains in use, one of the West's more popular tourist attractions and the setting for numerous Western movies.

Fire in 1889 destroyed most of Durango's earliest buildings, but many brick and stone structures from the early 1890s still stand. Railroad tickets are available at the **Durango and Silverton Depot** (479 Main Ave.), by phone (877-872-4607), or online. In the adjoining rail yard, a portion of the old Denver and Rio Grande roundhouse accommodates the twelve-thousand-square-foot **D&S Roundhouse Museum.** One of the early buildings not destroyed in the 1889 fire is the **Strater Hotel** (699 Main; 970-247-4431), opened in 1887. It remains in business. Operated by the La Plata County Historical Society in the 1904 Animas City School, the **Animas Museum** (3065 West 2nd Ave.; 970-259-2402) spotlights local history.

FAIRPLAY (PARK COUNTY)

It's fair to say Fairplay's evolution is convoluted. A gold rush town founded in 1859 in Colorado's mountain-surrounded South Park Basin, it got its equitable-sounding name from a group of miners who didn't think they'd gotten a fair shake in trying to stake claims around a prospecting camp on Tarryall Creek. They started calling that camp Grab-all, and when they found more gold farther west in the basin, they named their camp Fair Play. By 1861 the camp had grown into a town with a post office. But eight years later, Fair Play was renamed South Park. That held a few years until Fair Play came back into play. Finally, in 1924, postal officials decided the town's name should be one word.

Established in 1959 during Colorado's gold rush centennial, the **South Park Museum** (100 4th St.; 719-836-2387) is a complex of thirty-five restored gold rush–era buildings, some original to Fairplay, others moved in from ghost towns in the basin. Two are listed on the National Register of Historic Places. More than sixty thousand mining-era artifacts are displayed in the buildings, which are maintained by the South Park Historical Foundation.

FORT COLLINS (LARIMER COUNTY)

The city of Fort Collins traces to a military outpost called Camp Collins established on the Cache La Poudre River in 1862. When a flood destroyed the camp, it was relocated several miles downriver and designated as Fort Collins, which remained active to protect travelers along the Overland Trail until 1867. A small community that developed adjacent to the fort survived the army's departure and grew into an agricultural center and later one of the state's larger cities.

Fort Collins includes two National Historic Districts: Old Town Square, with twenty-two historic buildings, and the Avery House District of twenty-plus residences and buildings, including the 1879 **Franklin Avery House.** The visitor center (19 Old Town Square; 800-274-3678) has self-guided walking tours and material on other attractions.

Located in the city's 1904 Carnegie Library building, the **Fort Collins Museum of Discovery** (408 Mason Ct.; 970-221-6738) tells the city's story from the days of early exploration and French fur trappers forward.

FORT GARLAND (COSTILLA COUNTY)

When Fort Garland was established in 1858 to protect settlers in the San Luis Valley from Utes and Jicarilla Apaches, it was in New Mexico Territory. The post consisted of one-story adobe structures with three-foot walls (for insulation against harsh winters more than for defensive purposes) built around a rectangular parade ground. In May 1866, Kit Carson arrived with four companies of New Mexico Volunteers to assume command of the post. While there, the legendary scout was instrumental in negotiating a treaty with the Utes that would hold until 1879. Under the agreement, the Utes relocated to the southwestern quadrant of Colorado in exchange for a government payment of $60,000 a year for thirty years.

All was well with the Utes until miners began encroaching on Ute land following the discovery of gold in that part of Colorado. Following the Meeker Massacre in the fall of 1879 (see Meeker, Colorado), additional troops were rushed to Fort Garland. At one point, the post was overrun with fifteen companies, many of them having to live in tents during a brutal winter. Soldiers from the fort later escorted the Utes to new reservations in Utah and far southwestern Colorado.

After the confinement of the Utes to reservations, the army abandoned Fort Garland on November 30, 1883. The property went through a variety of owners, and by the late 1920s the old fort appeared doomed to demolition. But history-minded area residents raised enough money to buy the property and saved it. Plans to restore the remaining buildings were derailed by the Great Depression, and further delayed by World War II, but in 1945 the Colorado Historical Society acquired the site. By that time only five of the original twenty-two buildings still stood, but they were restored, and the **Fort Garland Museum** (29477 State Highway 159; 719-379-3512) opened in 1950.

GEORGETOWN (CLEAR CREEK COUNTY)

The Pike's Peak gold rush drew brothers George and David Griffith to Colorado from Kentucky, and in 1859 they founded Georgetown, the so-called "Silver Queen of the Rockies." Named for the older of the two siblings, the town did not truly boom until someone else discovered silver about eight miles away in 1864. Nearby Silver Plume developed as the typical rough mining camp, while Georgetown took the somewhat loftier path as a supply town and residential community. Georgetown continued to thrive until the silver market crashed in 1893. After that, the town did a slow fade until it gained new vitality as a tourist destination.

A monument to George Andrew Jackson stands at 320 Highway 103 just outside Idaho Springs, thirteen miles east of Georgetown off I-70. The Georgetown-Silver Plume National Historic District includes more than two hundred buildings and houses from the silver boom era. The **Georgetown Loop Railroad and Mining Park** (646 Loop Dr.; 888-456-6777) features a train excursion and tours of old mines.

The words "elegant" and "outhouse" do not normally appear in the same sentence, but one of the Old West's most elegant surviving outhouses stands outside the 1867–1879 **Hamill House** (305 Argentina St.). The six-seater was built in the Gothic Revival style with a cantilevered overhang, a ventilating cupola, and two entrances, truly a privy for the privileged. Built in 1867, the Hamill House was refurbished and enlarged by new owner William A. Hamill in 1879. The mine owner's restored Victorian residence is now a museum operated by Historic Georgetown, Inc. The nonprofit also maintains the adjacent **Alpine Hose No. 2 Fire Fighting Museum.**

The **Hotel de Paris Museum** (409 6th Ave.; 303-569-2311) is in the two-story former Hotel de Paris, opened in 1875. The **George Rowe Museum** (315 Main St., Silver Plume; 303-569-2562), housed in a two-story brick schoolhouse built in 1894, focuses on local history.

GLENWOOD SPRINGS (GARFIELD COUNTY)

The Ute Indians first realized the restorative power of the hot springs they called Yamapah, for "big medicine." A US Army officer noted the springs in 1860, but it was not until 1887 that Walter Devereux, a wealthy coal mine owner, bought land around the springs and began developing a health resort there that grew into Glenwood Springs.

The **Glenwood Springs Visitor Center** (802 Grand Ave.; 970-945-6580) has maps and brochures as well as a video on the town's history. The town's most imposing building is the 1893 **Hotel Colorado** (526 Pine St.; 970-945-6511), a resort hotel where notables like Buffalo Bill and President Theodore Roosevelt spent time.

Doc's Demise

When OK Corral participant "Doc" Holliday arrived in the new mountain resort town, he may have found some temporary comfort in the mineral-laden hot springs water, but no healing. Old beyond his years, the Georgia-born tubercular with a weakness for alcohol, gambling, and women rented a second-floor room in the luxurious Glenwood Springs Hotel in May 1887. It's the room he died in on November 8 that year, only thirty-six years old.

Fire destroyed Hotel Glenwood (732 Grand Ave.) in 1945. The more recent building standing at that location is home to a Doc Holliday museum operated by the Glenwood Springs Historical Society (970-945-9175). Still standing at 714 Grand Avenue is the old **Mirror Bar,** where Holliday liked to spend time when he was able. Holliday was buried in **Linnwood Cemetery** (Bennett Avenue and East 12th Street), but exactly where in the cemetery remains a mystery. There is a marker to him at GPS coordinates: N39° 32.38', W107° 19.23', placed in 2004, but no one knows how close it is to his actual burial place. A trail extending a half mile uphill from Bennett Avenue and East 12th Street leads to the cemetery, where signs point to the marker.

The **Frontier Museum** (1001 Colorado Ave.; 970-945-4448) occupies the 1905 Colonial Revival–style former residence of another notable Glenwood Springs medical practitioner—Dr. Marshall Dean. He had his medical office there as well until he moved to Denver in 1908. The house remained in the hands of its third owner's family until 1971, when it was donated to the local historical society for use as a museum.

GOLDEN (JEFFERSON COUNTY)

Founded in 1859 as a goldfield supply point, Golden was the territorial capital from 1862 to 1867 before it lost out to Denver. The town was named for early-day miner Tom Golden, not for all the precious metal extracted from the earth during Colorado's gold rush.

Opened in 1938 as the Jefferson County Museum, the **Golden Pioneer Museum and Park** (923 10th St.; 303-278-3557) refers to itself as a "cultural campus." It moved from its original location to its current home in 1996. The museum's collection includes more than sixteen thousand artifacts related to Golden's history.

Nineteen-year-old Thomas Pearce came from Cornwall, England, to Colorado in 1878 and worked as a hard-rock miner. In 1900, he and his wife Henrietta homesteaded in a valley between Golden and Central City. They grew vegetables, ran cattle, and raised eight children on their ranch. The Pearce Ranch remains in the family well over a century later, but in the 1990s, when a development threatened the original ranch house and related buildings, a community effort funded the dismantling and moving of the old structures to Golden. Starting in 1994, the ranch buildings—ranging from an 1870s log cabin to a vintage outhouse—were rebuilt there. Five years later, the **Golden History Park** (11th and Arapahoe; 303-278-3557) opened with the relocated old ranch as its centerpiece.

"At rest here by his request"

Wild West icon Buffalo Bill Cody was buried in 1917 on Lookout Mountain, with the Rocky Mountains on the west and the beginning of the Great Plains visible in the east. The inscription on his modest stone and concrete grave marker reads, "At rest here by his request." (Everyone expected that a much more impressive monument would be placed at the site, but that has not happened.) The notation about Cody being buried here "by his request" seems like a strange thing to point out, but the decision to bury Cody here was far from unanimous. The people of Cody, Wyoming, thought he should be laid to rest there, as did many in North Platte, Nebraska, where he was a resident longer than he was in Cody. Cody's widow Louisa and his closer friends said that Lookout Mountain had been his choice. Just in case, to prevent anyone from trying to dig Cody up for reburial, ten tons of concrete were poured over the grave. Four years later, when Louisa died, she was buried next to the old scout.

In 1921 Buffalo Bill's friend Johnny Baker founded the Buffalo Bill Memorial Museum. The first artifacts to go on display were the various objects Baker had gathered over the years, supplemented with things donated by Louisa Cody before her death. The City of Denver owned the museum site, but Baker and his wife Olive owned the artifacts and ran the museum and gift shop, which they called "Pahaska Tepee" for Cody's hunting lodge outside Yellowstone National Park. When Baker died in 1931, his widow continued to operate the museum until her death in 1956. Based on an earlier agreement, the collection and facilities became the property of the City of Denver, which continues to operate the museum (987 1/2 Lookout Mountain Rd.; 303-526-0744).

GRAND JUNCTION (MESA COUNTY)

Named because it was founded at the junction of the Colorado and Gunnison Rivers, Grand Junction also became a railroad junction, a major connecting point between Denver and Salt Lake City, in 1882. With the construction of dams, canals, and irrigation ditches, the valley grew as a major agricultural center.

Opened in 1966 and at its present location since 2000, the **Museum of Western Colorado** (462 Ute Ave.; 970-242-0971) covers a thousand years of western Colorado history. It also houses an extensive archival collection.

GRAND LAKE (GRAND COUNTY)

The dozen or more loud reports heard by Grand Lake residents on the night of July 4, 1883, had nothing to do with Independence Day. A bitter political rivalry, which began when the booming mining town sought to attain county seat status over the community of Hot Sulphur Springs, had festered to the point of assassination. Voters had opted for Grand Lake, but that did not diminish the antipathy of either side.

Shortly after pro-"Springs" county commissioners Barney Day and Edward P. Webber, accompanied by county clerk Thomas J. Dean, left Grand Lake's Fairview House Hotel that holiday evening, a party of masked men ambushed them near the natural lake that gave the town its name. In the gunfight that followed, Day killed one of the attackers but soon took a bullet in the heart. Before the other masked men escaped, Webber and Dean lay mortally wounded.

When someone pulled the bloody white mask off the man Day had killed, shocked bystanders saw it was another county commissioner, John Mills. Later that night, Sheriff Charles Royer and Undersheriff William Redman arrived to investigate the killings but made no arrests. In fact, they seemed completely baffled as to the identity of the perpetrators.

Since it was well known that Mills had belonged to the pro-"Lake" faction, it seemed clear the ambush had been pulled off by other Grand Lakers. But still there were no arrests. Later that summer, someone found Sheriff Royer dead of a single gunshot wound, an apparent suicide. On top of that, Undersheriff Redman had disappeared. No one was ever convicted in the murders of the county officials. Several years later, voters changed their minds and approved moving the county seat to Hot Sulphur Springs.

The Fairview House, where those wounded in the ambush later died, was razed in 1937. The graves of Day and Dean are on top of a hill on the west side of **Hot Sulphur Springs Cemetery** (just east of town off County Road 55; GPS coordinates: N40° 04.31', W106° 05.17').

Greeley (Weld County)

A newspaperman named this town after a newspaperman, and what a story lies behind that. It began with famed New York editor Horace Greeley, the journalist who offered some advice that has been quoted so often it became a cliché: "Go west, young man, go west." In addition to putting out the *New York Tribune* every day, Greeley aspired to create an agriculture-based utopian society or, as he wrote, "to plant a colony." In 1869 he organized a joint stock company to develop a society of moral, teetotaling, hard-working people. To lead the endeavor he chose Nathan Meeker, his agricultural editor. The company acquired acreage along the South Platte River valley and began recruiting colonists. Meeker arrived with 144 hand-picked families in April 1870 and set about transforming that part of the world. First known as Union Colony, Meeker renamed the settlement in honor of his boss. Colonists built a series of irrigation canals, plowed the prairie, and planted crops. Meeker was a driven man who pushed others just as hard—and sternly. The effort was a success, the beginning of one of the nation's fastest-growing cities. Later, Meeker would encounter different people, who wanted to live their way, not his. It cost him his life and the lives of nineteen others (see Meeker, Colorado).

The two-story adobe-brick house Meeker built for his family still stands at 1324 9th Avenue. It opened as a museum in 1929 and contains some of the original furnishings and other items that belonged to Meeker and his wife and children. The **Greeley History Museum** (714 8th St.; 970-350-9220) has more exhibits and artifacts related to Meeker, in addition to displays on other aspects of the city's story.

GUNNISON (GUNNISON COUNTY)

Unlike another well-known Western character called "Doc" (John Henry Holliday), "Doc" Shores was a good guy. Born Cyrus Wells Shores but nicknamed "Doc" in honor of the physician who delivered him, Shores spent most of his adult life as a lawman, from railroad bull to chief of police in Salt Lake City. In 1874, while serving as sheriff of Gunnison County, Shores captured alleged cannibal Alfred Packer (see Lake City, Colorado). Shores (1844–1934) is buried in **Gunnison Cemetery,** one mile east of Gunnison off US 50 (GPS coordinates: N38° 32.77', W106° 53.78').

IDAHO SPRINGS (CLEAR CREEK COUNTY)

The young nation's second great gold rush began in the winter of 1859 when prospector George Andrew Jackson discovered placer gold where Chicago Creek flowed into Clear Creek, not far from a spring that bubbled hot mineral water. Jackson tried to keep his find secret, but apparently it didn't occur to him that paying for supplies with gold dust would raise questions. Worse than that, it triggered a stampede as other prospectors descended on the area. The mining camp that developed here was first known as Jackson's Diggings, but the hot springs came to be called Idaho Springs, and the town eventually took that name as well. Soon, rich veins of gold were found on the rocky slopes of Clear Creek Canyon, and hard-rock mining began in the area.

Idaho Springs has six buildings and one bridge listed on the National Register of Historic Places, in addition to the commercial district, which includes forty-six vintage buildings. The **Idaho Springs Heritage Museum** (2060 Miner St.; 303-567-4382) tells how the Colorado gold rush began here. The museum, located in the old James and Lucy Undersell house, is operated by the Historical Society of Idaho Springs. A self-guided historic site walking tour is available at the visitor center that's part of the museum.

In 1909, a monument to Jackson was erected near where he first found gold, commemorating the centennial of his discovery. An enormous boulder on a concrete base with interpretive plaques, the monument stands in the parking lot of the former Idaho Springs middle school (GPS coordinates: N39° 44.36', W105° 31.38').

One of the town's most prolific mines—producing some $100 million in gold—was the Argo, which operated until 1943. Listed on the National Register of Historic Places, the **Argo Mill and Tunnel** (2350 Riverside Dr.; 303-567-2421) has a mining museum and offers mine shaft tours. The **Phoenix Mine** (830 Trail Creek Rd.; 303-567-0422) also provides tours.

JULESBURG (SEDGWICK COUNTY)

For more than two decades, Julesburg was a town on the move—literally. Named for Jules Beni, who established a trading post on the south side of the Platte River in 1859, it served as a stop for both the Overland Stage Company and the Pony Express. In February 1865, Cheyenne and Lakota Indians raided the place and burned it to the ground. The year before, a military post was established about a mile south of the Platte at Lodgepole Creek. Following the Indian attack, a new Julesburg arose six miles east of its first location so as to be protected by the fort. Julesburg continued as a stagecoach stop until the Union Pacific Railroad arrived in June 1867 and the town pulled up stakes again to be on the mainline. Julesburg became a classic rough railroad town and prospered as a shipping point even after the railroad pushed farther west. The town was relocated in 1881 to its fourth and final location, the junction of the United Pacific mainline and new trackage connecting to Denver. The old Union Pacific Railroad depot now houses the **Depot Museum** (201 West 1st St.; 970-474-2264), featuring exhibits on the Pony Express and Union Pacific memorabilia, as well as early-day relics.

Established as Camp Rankin, Julesburg's Fort Sedgwick was renamed in honor of Civil War hero General John Sedgwick. The soldiers stationed there protected the mail and passenger route that followed the South Platte River and later the Union Pacific work crews. The post was abandoned in 1871 but got a boost in name recognition when "Fort Sedgwick" was featured prominently in the 1990 Oscar-winning Kevin Costner film *Dances with Wolves*. Since nothing remained of the real fort, the movie was filmed elsewhere. The **Fort Sedgwick Museum** (114 East 1st St.; 970-474-2061) features relics and artifacts that contributed to the history of Julesburg and Sedgwick County.

Pony Express Statue

Twenty-six miles of the Pony Express route cut through northeastern Colorado, and Julesburg was one of only two stopping places in what was then Colorado Territory. In 2002, a larger-than-life bronze statue of a Pony Express rider was placed outside the Fort Sedgwick Museum, only a thousand feet from the old trail. La Junta artist Brenda Daniher sculpted the piece.

LAKE CITY (HINSDALE COUNTY)

Lake City, named for nearby Lake San Cristobal—Colorado's second-largest natural lake—began in 1875 as a supply point for miners.

Nothing even remotely funny occurred when erstwhile guide Alfred Packer and five gold seekers got trapped in a blizzard near future Lake City in the winter of 1874. Not only were the prospectors doomed, but during the following century their fates would inspire a cornucopia of tasteless jokes.

With less than a two-week supply of food, the party—against all advice—ventured into the San Juan Mountains on February 9 in search of gold. That spring, Packer emerged from the mountains to report that the other five men had died. When authorities went to their campsite to bury the dead, they found evidence of cannibalism. Whether Packer killed the miners to eat them, or they died of natural causes and then were eaten continues to be debated, but Packer was jailed and charged with murder. Before he went to trial, he escaped and was not recaptured until 1883. Tried for murder and convicted, he was sentenced to forty years in prison. Pardoned in 1900, he died in 1907.

The campsite and grave of the five men Packer guided to their deaths is two and a half miles from Lake City off State Highway 149 (GPS coordinates: N38° 00.01', W107° 17.70'). The Ladies Union Aid Society had a railing built around the mass grave of the victims in the summer of 1928 and placed an explanatory plaque on a large rock. The Jazz Age marker does not mention cannibalism, but as one online writer later put it, a modern interpretive sign "fleshes out the story with . . . meaty details."

Packer is buried in **Littleton Cemetery** (2552 West Ridge Ct., Littleton). He has a standard marble military veteran's marker, giving only his name and his unit, Company F, Sixteenth US Infantry.

Two Colorado museums have exhibits and artifacts related to Packer: the **Hinsdale County Museum** (130 North Silver St.; 970-944-2050) and the **Museum of Western Colorado** (462 Ute Ave., Grand Junction; 970-242-0971). This museum holds firearms that belonged to Packer and displays a small axe and a fragment from a human skull found at the campsite during an archaeological investigation.

LEADVILLE (LAKE COUNTY)
Placer gold mining followed by hard-rock mining produced a modest amount of gold in the vicinity of future Leadville in the 1860s, but the discovery of a rich lode of silver-bearing lead carbonate is what led to the birth and wild youth of Leadville. From 1877 until the silver market crashed in 1893, Leadville measured up as one of the Wild West's wildest boomtowns. During that time, it was an easy place to make money, but at ten-thousand-plus feet above sea level, it was a

hard place to live. (It remains the nation's highest incorporated city.) Winters here were off-the-chart miserable, and snow was possible even in the dog days of summer.

But none of that made much difference to the thousands of miners and all the other standard boomtown characters who ascended to Leadville. At its peak, the town reached a population estimated at thirty thousand. After the silver market meltdown, a short-lived upswing in gold mining followed by lead and zinc mining kept Leadville alive, though barely.

A seventy-square-block National Historic District includes numerous Victorian structures. A self-guided downtown walking tour is available at local museums and the **Leadville and Lake County Chamber of Commerce** (809 Harrison Ave.). A little more than a block away stands the 1886 **Delaware Hotel** (700 Harrison Ave.). Leadville has eight museums—on a per capita basis, the most museums of any Colorado community. Two of those museums, the **Heritage Museum** (102 East 9th St.; 719-486-1878) and the **National Mining Hall of Fame and Museum** (120 West 9th St.; 719-486-1229) focus on Leadville and its economic engine.

The **Tabor Home Museum** (116 East 5th St.; 719-293-2391) is devoted to Horace Austin Warner Tabor, one of the Wild West's more notable figures. A prospector turned retailer turned extremely wealthy silver mine owner, Tabor and his first wife lived in this two-story clapboard house for four years before moving to Denver amid scandal after Tabor left his first wife for a much younger woman. The Leadville house originally stood at 312 Harrison Street but was moved to make room for the **Tabor Opera House** (308 Harrison St.; 719-486-8409). Built in 1879, the three-story brick Italianate-style opera house hosted performances by some of the best-known entertainers of the late nineteenth and early twentieth centuries. The City of Leadville purchased the building in 2016, and it is maintained by a nonprofit foundation. Performers still appear on a stage that in the past accommodated noted personages ranging from Buffalo Bill Cody to Oscar Wilde to five circus tigers. A final structure connected to Tabor is the **Tabor Grand Hotel** (701 Harrison St.). The hotel accommodated guests until it closed in 1989. Within only a few years it had fallen into serious disrepair and was in danger of being razed when, with private and public funding, it was restored and reopened as low-income housing and ground-level retail space.

Mart Duggan

Born in Ireland in 1848, Mart Duggan immigrated to the US with his parents and grew up in New York's Irish slums. That toughened him to the extent that he fit right in when he left for the Colorado goldfields during the Civil War. Duggan tried mining in the Georgetown area but didn't have any luck, so he became a bouncer at one of the local saloons. Though capable of taking care of himself with his fists, a six-shooter had a longer reach. After putting several bullets in a man in what was adjudged a clear case of self-defense, he moved on to Leadville in 1878. When newly elected mayor Horace Tabor appointed the city's first marshal, the lawman soon thought it best for his career—and longevity—to relocate. The second marshal was shot and killed not long after taking office. Leadville's third marshal was Duggan, who proved quite effective until April 19, 1889, when someone shot him to death outside one of the city's many watering holes. No one was ever charged with the murder, but the man generally suspected of having been paid to do it was later killed in South America.

Duggan's remains were taken to Denver for burial in **Riverside Cemetery** (5201 Brighton Rd., Denver, block 2, lot 41). If Duggan ever had a headstone, it has disappeared. In 2010, a memorial monument with details on his life and death was placed at the grave site.

"My Wife . . . Jane Kirkham . . ."

Many a lonesome tombstone dots the vastness of the once wild West, but few pose as many unanswered questions as the grave marker near the old Leadville–Buena Vista stagecoach road. Located east of the Arkansas River near a rock ledge, it bears this inscription: "My Wife—Jane Kirkham, Died March 7, 1879 Aged 38 years, 3 months, 7 days[.]"

The most fanciful tale connected to the stone holds that Mrs. Kirkham's husband shot her to death in a most bizarre manner. Supposedly, Mr. Kirkham (first name unknown) was a deputy sheriff assigned to guard the Leadville stage from road agents. With Kirkham riding incognito on the stage, a masked gunman stepped out from the rocks and ordered it to halt. The deputy killed the bandit, only to discover to his horror that the would-be robber was his wife, dressed as a man. It would have been sensational newspaper fare, but there are no contemporary accounts of such an event. Nor have researchers been able to identify a deputy named Kirkham or anyone named Jane Kirkham living in the area at that time.

A more mundane theory has Mrs. Kirkham as a stagecoach passenger who died in childbirth. But either scenario begs the question of why her husband buried her on the spot and then had a tombstone hauled back to her grave. Why not just take her body to town for burial? The findagrave.com entry for Jane gives her full name as Jane Harris Kirkham and lists her husband as Benjamin F. Kirkham. While this appears to be the work of a knowledgeable descendant, no explanation for her death is offered. The tombstone is fifteen miles south of Leadville, just north of the junction of US 24 and State Highway 82. However, the site is on the other side of the Arkansas River, below a rock outcropping. The marker can be seen with binoculars.

MEEKER (RIO BLANCO COUNTY)

Meeker was an unplanned town, born of tragedy. In 1879, Nathan Meeker, the newspaper editor who founded the agricultural colony that became Greeley, was appointed agent of the White River Indian Agency in northwestern Colorado. Having been successful in transforming prairie lands to potato fields in the South Platte River valley, Meeker thought he could convert the White River Utes to farmers. To that end, he plowed a tract the Utes considered sacred and otherwise tried to force white ways on them.

Realizing by their reaction that he may have pushed too hard, Meeker asked for military backup. A contingent under Maj. Thomas Thornbush rode south from Fort Fred Steele, Wyoming, toward the reservation. Learning of the approaching soldiers, the Utes believed their sovereignty had been violated, and they hadn't been all that happy with their treatment in the first place. The Indians attacked, and in the lengthy fighting that followed, known as the Milk Creek Battle, ten soldiers were killed, including Thornbush.

After the fight, the Utes attacked the agency. They killed Meeker and nine agency employees and captured his wife, one of his children, and several others. The outbreak led to the tribe's forcible removal to reservations in Utah and the southwestern corner of Colorado.

To get control of the situation, the army sent in more troops and established a camp at the burned-out agency. When the post was abandoned in 1883, the military sold the buildings. Purchased by new arrivals eager to settle the recently opened land, those log cabins seeded a town named for the slain Meeker.

A Game Warden Thwarts a Bank Robbery

Colorado deputy game warden W.H. Clark had been commissioned to enforce the state's nascent conservation laws. He spent his time looking for poachers or people fishing out of season, but on October 13, 1896, Clark and several other Meeker citizens thwarted a bank robbery.

Clark probably didn't see the three men walk into the J.W. Hugus General Mercantile, which housed the local bank, but when he heard a couple of gunshots from inside, he immediately realized what was afoot. Running to get his rifle, he alerted others and began organizing citizens to foil the robbery. Seeing three horses tied just outside the bank's back door, the warden correctly surmised the robbers would be coming out that way and directed most of the armed townsfolk to come with him to cover the back of the building while he dispatched others to watch the front.

Soon, three bandits emerged, marching everyone who had been inside ahead of them as human shields. When Clark shouldered his rifle, one of the men saw the gun go up and shot the game warden in the chest. As Clark fell, the hostages bolted, leaving the robbers unprotected. Bullets came from every direction and the robbers went down. Two died on the spot; the third lived only a few hours.

According to differing accounts, the shots that alerted Clark had either been fired by one of the robbers to emphasize their resolve or by accident. Whatever happened, the bandits should have made a run for it then, but they lingered to collect the money.

The bodies of the robbers, later identified as George Law, Billy Olmstead, and Jim Shirley, were displayed and photographed before they were buried in the local cemetery. Clark, though seriously wounded, recovered and went on to a long and respected career in Colorado.

The three bandits are buried in **Highland Cemetery** (off County Road 4, a half mile south of Meeker). The **White River Museum** (565 Park Ave.; 970-878-9982) in Meeker has exhibits and artifacts related to the Meeker Massacre, the development of the town, and the botched bank robbery, including a hotel register signed by Jim Shirley.

MONTROSE (MONTROSE COUNTY)

Founded in 1882, Montrose was a supply point for area mining camps. Later it evolved as a cattle town and agricultural center.

Montrose's **Ute Indian Museum** (17253 Chipeta Dr.; 970-249-3098) has one of the nation's best collections of cultural materials related to the Utes. Located on the 8.65-acre homestead of Chief Ouray, the Ute leader who tried to help his people by adapting to white ways, the museum complex includes a memorial park dedicated to the chief and his wife Chipeta, her crypt, and a memorial to the Spanish explorers who came through the area in the eighteenth century.

Museum of the Mountain West

Private museums are often for-profit ventures operated by people with only a layperson's knowledge of history. But the **Museum of the Mountain West** (68169 East Miami Rd.; 970-240-3400), while it started in 1997 as a privately owned attraction, was founded as a labor of love by Richard E. Fike, a retired professional archaeologist who began collecting Old West artifacts before he started first grade. The museum is a collection of vintage Western structures moved in from other areas, with some buildings newly constructed with old logs or lumber. Inside each are Western artifacts. In 2005, the Fikes created a nonprofit entity to take over the museum, though he continued as its director. The museum is two miles east of Montrose.

OURAY (OURAY COUNTY)

The Utes, understandably, were not happy when prospectors and miners descended on their high-country lands when silver and gold ore were found in great quantity in the San Juan Mountains of southwestern Colorado. Consequently, the decision in 1877 to name the state's latest mining boomtown after Ute chief Ouray must have seemed like no consolation at all.

Ten years later, the Denver and Rio Grande Railroad began serving the town, and it enjoyed even more prosperity until mining declined in the area. Billing itself as "America's Switzerland," Ouray became a popular resort community. More than one hundred films have been made in the area, many of them classic Westerns such as *How the West Was Won* and *True Grit*.

One of the better preserved of the old Colorado mining towns, the entire town of Ouray is listed on the National Register of Historic Places. The **Ouray Visitor Center** (1230 Main St.; 970-325-4746) offers a self-guided walking tour of the historic district. The **Ouray County Museum** (420 6th Ave.; 970-325-4576) is located in the old St. Joseph's Miner's Hospital, a two-story stone building opened in 1887. The **Wright Opera House** (472 Main St.; 970-325-4399) was built by brothers Ed and George Wright in 1888 because Ed and his wife Letitia wanted the residents of Ouray to have a decent alternative to the town's saloons, dance halls, bordellos, and gambling dens. All of those types of places mostly disappeared when mining in the area ended, but the opera house is still entertaining locals and visitors. Two among many additional vintage buildings in Ouray are the 1887–1886 **Beaumont Hotel** (505 Main St.) and the 1888 **Ouray County Courthouse** (541 4th St.). The **Ouray County Ranch History Museum** (321 Sherman St.; 970-316-1085) is located eleven miles northwest of Ouray in Ridgway, Colorado.

PLATTEVILLE (WELD COUNTY)

Platteville was founded in 1871 on the east bank of the South Platte River in northern Colorado and incorporated sixteen years later. But long before the town came into being, two pioneer entrepreneurs—Pierre "Louis" Vasquez and Andrew Sublette—established a fur trading post here in 1835.

Located roughly halfway between Bent's Fort (near La Junta) on the south and Fort William (later known as Fort Laramie) on the north, the trading post came to be known as Fort Vasquez. Built of adobe, it was one hundred feet square and had walls two feet thick. Exchanging manufactured goods for buffalo hides brought in by the Cheyenne and Arapaho Indians, at its high point the fort accommodated nearly two dozen traders plus workers who performed various tasks.

Despite cutthroat competition Vasquez and Sublette ran the trading post for seven years before selling it in 1842. After that, the old fort saw a variety of uses, from stagecoach stop to temporary military encampment to church. In 1934 the ranching family on whose land the old fort stood deeded what remained of the trading post to the county, and with funding from the Works Progress Administration, a smaller replica of the fort was constructed and opened to the public in 1937. The Colorado Historical Society (History Colorado today) took over the site in the 1950s, and during the following two decades oversaw extensive archaeological work. In 2005 the fort underwent a major restoration. The **Fort Vasquez Museum** (13412 US 85; 970-785-2832) has exhibits relating to the fur trade, the fort, and the Plains Indians. The **Pioneer Museum** (502 Madison; 970-381-1105) focuses on the history of Platteville and Weld County.

PUEBLO (PUEBLO COUNTY)

On the Arkansas River in southern Colorado, Pueblo evolved from an 1830s log trading post to a fortified adobe trading post and plaza known as El Pueblo and then to a mining, railroad, and manufacturing center. Beginning in 1821, when Mexico won its independence from Spain, the Arkansas River at this point marked the boundary between Mexico and US territory.

The **Pueblo Convention and Visitors Bureau** (302 North Santa Fe Ave.; 719-542-1704) has self-guided walking tours and information on Pueblo historic sites. **El Pueblo History Center** (301 North Union Ave.; 719-583-0453) includes a replica of an 1840s trading post and remnants of the original trading post that stood at the site.

Located in the 1924 Denver and Rio Grande Western Railroad freight depot, the **Pueblo Heritage Center** (201 West B St.; 719-295-1517) tells the story of Pueblo, once known as the Steel City of the West. The town's one-time steel-making industry contributed to Pueblo's other two economic mainstays: mining and railroading. The Pueblo Heritage Center also has an exhibit on the city's saddle-making history, including a collection of saddle-making equipment from the Frazier Saddle Company's former shop.

Pueblo once had more saddle-makers than anyplace in the Old West. In fact, the Pueblo Heritage Society calls Pueblo the one-time saddle-making capital of the world. Pioneer saddle-makers such as S.G. Gallup, Robert Thomas Frazier, and Tom Flynn popularized the Pueblo-style saddle, notable for its high pommel, high back, and double rigging. Their innovation, which transformed the all-important piece of tack from uncomfortable and unstable to just the opposite, became the standard across the West. Gallup opened the first shop in Pueblo in 1870, followed by Flynn in 1892. Frazier (1850–1931), a former deputy sheriff who served in booming Leadville during its wild heyday, had been working with Gallup since 1880 but opened his own shop in 1898. One of his first big customers was the Miller Brothers' 101 Ranch Wild West Show. Still owned by the Frazier family, the company continued in operation until 1958. The Fraziers' two friendly competitors, the shop started by Gallup and Flynn's saddle shop, remained in business until 1928 and 1935, respectively.

Robert Thomas Frazier's house, privately owned, still stands at 2121 Elizabeth Street. He is buried in **Roselawn Cemetery** (1706 Roselawn Rd.).

Lucky the Horse

What wooden Indians were to early-day cigar stores, papier mâché horses were to saddle shops. But while cigar store Indians served only as ornamentation, saddle-makers used the faux horses for fitting saddles. One such horse stood in Thomas Flynn's shop until June 3, 1921, when floodwater inundated the business. Found the following morning lodged in a cottonwood tree fifteen miles downstream, the horse became known as Lucky. In 1989, by then on display at a different business, Lucky made it through a fire that destroyed the store. Now Lucky is a permanent fixture at the Pueblo Heritage Center, still on the job displaying a Pueblo-made saddle.

Rock Canyon Ranch

Texas cattleman Charles Goodnight did not like spending money *unnecessarily*. In 1866, he and partner Oliver Loving pushed a herd of longhorns from Fort Belknap, Texas, to Denver, via Pueblo. Goodnight liked what he saw around Pueblo and decided to settle there, but before then, he and Loving developed what came to be called the Goodnight-Loving Trail from Texas to Colorado.

On their first trail drive, they had used "Uncle" Dick Wooten's toll road through Raton Pass, but on the next drive, Goodnight balked at paying a quarter a man and a nickel a head for his cattle to use the road and blazed his own trail to the east of the pass. On their next drive, Loving suffered a mortal wound while staving off an attack by Comanches and later died near Fort Sumner, New Mexico. Goodnight finished the trail drive but then returned to Fort Sumner, had his business associate and friend's body exhumed, and took his casket back to Texas and his final resting place. Writer Larry McMurtry later used the incident in his 1986 Pulitzer Prize–winning novel *Lonesome Dove*.

Goodnight established the **Rock Canyon Ranch** (State Highway 96 and Siloam Road; 719-250-9435) in a canyon along the Arkansas River just west of Pueblo in 1869. The restored stone barn that Goodnight built around 1870 was listed on the National Register of Historic Places in 1974. Considered one of Colorado's most significant historic structures related to ranching, the old barn is owned by the City of Pueblo and curated by the nonprofit Goodnight Barn Preservation, Inc. Goodnight operated the Rock Canyon Ranch until 1876 when he moved to the Texas Panhandle and took up ranching there.

One of the Wild West's more unusual incidents played out in and around Pueblo—a legal battle between the Santa Fe Railroad and the Denver and Rio Grande Railroad that nearly escalated into a shooting war. When the discovery of a rich silver lode turned Leadville into a boomtown in 1879, the two railroads fought over right-of-way through Royal Gorge, a point northwest of Pueblo where the Arkansas River flowed through a long, narrow canyon flanked by one-thousand-foot cliffs. Only thirty feet wide, the gorge had room for only one set of tracks. When the Santa Fe reached the gorge and started laying track, the Denver and Rio Grande built a series of stone fortifications along the river and began harassing its competitor by rolling down boulders, throwing Santa Fe tools in the river, and other means. Soon, both sides employed private armies to defend their interests.

While lawyers argued in the courts, the dispute climaxed in Pueblo, where sixty-plus hired gunman, under Ford County, Kansas, sheriff Bat Masterson, representing the Santa Fe, were confronted by a larger force of law enforcement officers and special deputies there on behalf of the Denver and Rio Grande. Masterson's men had fortified themselves in the Santa Fe roundhouse, supplementing their small-arms firepower with a cannon commandeered from the local armory. They eventually gave up when Masterson became convinced that a court order giving the Denver and Rio Grande the right-of-way it wanted was legitimate.

Adjacent to Pueblo's 1889 Union Station, the **Pueblo Railway Museum** (200 West B St.; 719-544-1773) focuses on the five railroad lines that once served the city. **Royal Gorge Bridge and Park** (4218 County Road 3A, Cañon City; 888-333-5597) is the highest suspension bridge in North America and spans 956 feet over the Arkansas River.

ST. ELMO (CHAFFEE COUNTY)

When mining began in this part of the Sawatch Range in 1880, the community that developed was named St. Elmo after the hugely popular 1866 novel by August Jane Evans. The town reached its high point in the 1890s with some two thousand residents and all the amenities of a mining town, from hotels and stores to saloons and dance halls.

St. Elmo declined as the mines around it began to fail in the early twentieth century. The downward slide gained avalanche-like momentum when the town lost rail service in 1922 and the last operating mine closed. When the postmaster died in 1952, the government shuttered the post office and St. Elmo became a ghost town. With more than two score vintage structures, St. Elmo is a ghost town that looks like a ghost town.

Twenty miles southwest of Buena Vista, the nearest small town to St. Elmo is Nathrop. From there, go south three-tenths of a mile to County Road 162 and follow it 15.4 miles to St. Elmo. The **St. Elmo General Store** (25865 County Road 162, Nathrop) is the only operating business, open in the summer months.

SILVERTON (SAN JUAN COUNTY)

Prospectors found placer gold in the San Juan Mountains in 1860, but the Ute Indians resisted any influx of miners, and no production began in the area until 1870. Another four years passed before significant mining took off. When the Denver and Rio Grande Railroad reached Silverton in 1882, the town's future was assured—at least for as long as the gold lasted. Most of the mines in the area played out by the 1910s, and a couple that did continue to operate into the modern era eventually flooded. Tourism evolved as the town's leading industry, but Silverton's boom days had passed. Declared a National Historic Site in 1961, much of the town's nineteenth- and early twentieth-century architecture still stands.

Many visitors arrive via the Durango and Silverton Railroad, but there's also the so-called Million Dollar Highway. On the map as US 550, the highway began as a toll road in 1883. It's an incredibly scenic but winding route that supposedly got its nickname when someone who had just traveled it swore they would never do so again, even for a "million dollars."

Silverton town marshal Clayton Ogsbury had only been on the job three months when the La Plata County sheriff sought his help in arresting two outlaws who had escaped from jail in Durango. As Ogsbury, the sheriff, and another lawman approached the Diamond Saloon in Silverton, one of the outlaws shot and killed the marshal.

Then both wanted men started blazing away at the other two lawmen, forcing them to pull back. Outraged citizens soon caught the pair and lynched them. The shooting occurred outside the **Diamond Saloon** (11th and Greene Street). Dedicated in 2016, a historical plaque on the building standing there today tells the story. Marshal Ogsbury (1847–1881) was buried in Hillside Cemetery, but his family later had his remains exhumed and buried in Guilderland Cemetery, Altamont, New York.

From the first funeral in 1875, about three thousand people have been buried in **Hillside Cemetery.** Contrary to its name, this twenty-acre cemetery is located on the side of Boulder Mountain, a little north of the courthouse. The graves reflect the cultural diversity of all mining towns, with many foreign-born workers and family members buried here. Every gravestone tells a story. For instance, there's the final resting place of the unfortunate Peter Dalla. A saloonkeeper, he fell in love and asked his lady fair for her hand in marriage. She said yes, but her other lover took exception to their nuptial plans. When shooting Dalla twice didn't work, on September 16, 1904, someone used dynamite to blow up the groom-to-be's residence and the wedding was permanently off.

Built in 1882–1883 by perfume importer and mill owner W.S. Thomson, the three-story granite Grand Hotel (the "Imperial" in its name came later) was Silverton's most imposing building, and still is. In addition to accommodating visitors, for a quarter century the hotel's second floor held the town and county's offices, making the Grand both a hotel and city hall–courthouse. Like many Old West hotels that managed to survive fire or the wrecking ball, the hotel eventually closed and fell into disrepair. But as Silverton's tourist industry grew, new owners restored the **Grand Imperial Hotel** (1219 Greene St.; 970-387-5527) to its original elegance and reopened it.

Organized in 1964, the San Juan County Historical Society has done much to preserve Silverton's history and its late Victorian architecture. Starting in the mid-1980s the society began an ambitious effort to open a museum and acquire and stabilize historic properties. The society's holdings include the 1902 county jail, the mountainside Old 100 Boarding House at the Old 100 Mine, the 1906 Silverton power station, and one of the West's oldest newspapers, the *Silverton Standard and Miner*. The **Mining Heritage Center** museum complex (1557 Greene St.; 970-387-5609) is adjacent to the courthouse.

The Mayflower Mill, and others like it in mining towns across the Old West, did not grind wheat or corn. Technically, this 1929 industrial site is a stamp mill, the place where ore was broken up for conversion into gold or base metals like copper and zinc. The historical society saved the mill from demolition after the area's last mine closed in 1991. The **Mayflower Mill** (135 County Road 2; 970-387-0294) is two miles northeast of Silverton. Tickets to view the mill are available at the Mining Heritage Center.

STERLING (LOGAN COUNTY)

Despite all the silver found in Colorado, the name of this town has nothing to do with precious metal. Instead, it was named for Sterling, Illinois. Its post office opened in 1874 to serve an agricultural community that had developed about four miles north of the South Platte River, but when the Union Pacific Railroad entered Logan County in 1881, the community moved to its current location to be adjacent to the tracks. The town stands on the site of an Overland Trail trading post that had a much more attention-grabbing name than Sterling: Fort Wicked.

Built to resemble an early-day trading post, the **Overland Trail Museum** (110 Overland Trail; 970-522-3895) opened in 1936. Much expanded over the years, the museum complex includes several restored historic structures and a separate building with exhibits focusing on the story of rural electrification.

TELLURIDE (SAN MIGUEL COUNTY)

Mining developed in this area in 1875, and by 1880 a vigorous town called Columbia was booming. Columbia was changed to Telluride when the town sought a post office and the government said there was already a Columbia in California. Telluride was a semi–ghost town when it reinvented itself as a ski resort in the 1970s.

Downtown Telluride, with numerous historic buildings, was named a National Historic District in 1964. The **Telluride Historical Museum** (201 West Gregory Ave.; 970-728-3344) tells the town's story.

Mineral production around Telluride eventually declined, but the local economy was still quite healthy on June 24, 1889, when three men robbed the local bank and escaped with around $20,000. Many believe that one of the robbers was Robert LeRoy Parker, soon to be much better known as Butch Cassidy. The San Miguel Valley Bank stood at 131 West Colorado Avenue. Burned in 1892, it was replaced by the Mahr Building. A historical plaque marks the site.

Tin Cup (Gunnison County)

The people who lived in this gold mining town were all about making money—legally or illegally—but they did not lack civic pride. When their boomtown was incorporated as Virginia City in 1859, the people didn't like it. Both Montana and Nevada already had a Virginia City, and there was even another Virginia City in Colorado. Someone suggested Tin Cup, a name inspired by the story of a miner who had collected a tin coffee cup full of gold dust in the vicinity. The Post Office Department went along with the idea, and the community had a much more evocative and appropriate name.

Early on Tin Cup runneth over with con men, gamblers, claim jumpers, robbers, and hard cases who would kill whether a fellow needed killing or not. Consequently, the community proved hard on law enforcement. Of seven men who served as peace officers in the town's first three years, three were shot to death, one traded his badge for a Bible and joined the clergy, and another was said to have ended up in an insane asylum. Folklore holds that the standing advice given a new officer was "See nothing, hear nothing, do nothing. The first arrest you make will be your last."

Even a clever name couldn't keep a town alive when the minerals played out, and from a high point of around six thousand people, Tin Cup emptied and by 1918 was a ghost town. During its heyday, the Tin Cup mining area yielded more than $7 million in gold.

To reach Tin Cup, from Gunnison, travel north 10.1 miles on State Highway 135 to County Road 742. Follow County Road 742 for 22.9 miles to County Road 55 and then 1.9 miles to Tin Cup. Harry Rivers, one of the marshals killed in the line of duty in Tin Cup in 1882, is buried in the center of Tin Cup Cemetery.

TRINIDAD (LAS ANIMAS COUNTY)

Trinidad grew from a well-used stopover point on the Santa Fe Trail. South-bound travelers could fill their water barrels from the Purgatoire River and rest before beginning the hard climb over Raton Pass. By 1860, a few adobe and log structures stood at the campsite, and a year later residents began laying out a town, a segment of the well-worn trail becoming Main Street. The government approved a post office for Trinidad in 1863. By 1867 five stagecoaches a week stopped at Trinidad, but no significant development took place until the Denver and Rio Grande Railroad began moving south from Pueblo. Its tracks stopped at El Moro, a few miles southeast of Trinidad, but when the Atchison, Topeka and Santa Fe cut through Trinidad on its way to Santa Fe in 1878, the town's future was assured, and the Denver and Rio Grande soon extended its line from El Moro to Trinidad.

Bat Masterson and his friends Wyatt Earp and Doc Holliday all spent some time in Trinidad in the early 1880s. None of them were involved in any gunplay while in town, but the city did see some typical Wild West shootings, including the wild April 16, 1882, gunfight that left gambler Frank "Cockeyed" Loving mortally wounded.

The National Historic Landmark District downtown has 143 nineteenth-century buildings. A self-guided walking tour is available at the **Trinidad Welcome Center** (309 Nevada; 791-846-9512). Loving's grave has been lost. While in Trinidad as city marshal in 1882–1883, Masterson had an office on the top floor of the Grand

Columbian Hotel. Though no longer a hotel, the building still stands at the northwest corner of Main and Commercial Streets.

The **Trinidad Historical Museum** (312 East Main St.; 719-846-7217) complex includes the restored 1870 adobe Felipe Baca House, the 1882 Victorian mansion where cattle baron Frank Bloom and his wife lived, a re-created Victorian garden, and the **Santa Fe Trail Museum.** That museum's collection includes a buckskin jacket that belonged to Kit Carson.

Kit Carson Statue

By 1903, famed scout Kit Carson had been dead thirty-five years, but some who knew him still lived, including Daniel L. Taylor. A former Trinidad mayor, Taylor donated eight acres for a city park to be named for Carson and began a subscription drive to raise funds for a statue of the frontiersman. Once enough money had been collected, two sculptors were commissioned to produce a heroic bronze. August Lukeman used photographs to sculpt Carson. The other artist, Frederick Roth, sculpted the horse. Mounted on a sixty-plus-ton granite base, the statue was dedicated June 1, 1913. It is regarded as one of the finest equestrian statues in the nation. The statue stands in **Kit Carson Park** (Kansas Avenue and San Pedro Street).

VIRGINIA DALE (LARIMER COUNTY)

Jack Slade may have been a disreputable sort (see Salt Lake City, Utah), but he thought enough of his wife Virginia Dale to name the Overland Trail stage stop he ran after her. Built in 1862, the one-story log structure accommodated thousands of west-bound travelers who stopped here, including Mark Twain when he was still Samuel Clemens, a young man headed to the Nevada mining boomtown of Virginia City. Later, as Twain, he wrote of his experience in *Roughing It*. Refurbished with grant money by the Virginia Dale Community Club, the stagecoach stop is the best-preserved structure connected with the Overland Trail still at its original location.

The ghost town of Virginia Dale is forty-five miles north of Fort Collins on US 287, only four miles south of the Wyoming state line. The old Virginia Dale stagecoach station is one mile east of US 287 at the end of County Road 43F. A historical marker stands where the county road intersects the highway. The station is on private property but visible from the public road.

Wray (Yuma County)

In September 1868, under the command of Maj. George Forsyth, fifty civilian scouts accompanied by a small detachment of soldiers left Fort Wallace in Kansas in search of hostile Cheyennes. Marching deeply into Indian-held land and finding ample sign of their presence, the overconfident but undersized force took it as good news. On September 16 they made camp on the Arikaree Fork of the Republican River, just across the Kansas border in Colorado. The next morning a large Cheyenne war party under Roman Nose attacked. Under withering fire, the soldiers and scouts withdrew to a sandbar in the river that afforded better cover. Forsyth dispatched some of the scouts to ride to Fort Wallace for help. Before the war party withdrew, when a relief column showed up, an estimated twenty-three Cheyennes (including Roman Nose) and five soldiers had been killed. One of the soldiers was Lt. Frederick Beecher, and the sandbar where the command stood off the Indians came to be known as Beecher's Island.

The brutal siege is now known as the Battle of Beecher Island. Lt. Col. George Armstrong Custer called the standoff that began September 17, 1868, the greatest Indian battle on the plains, but then, as his subsequent campaign along the Little Bighorn in Montana Territory would show, his judgment was not always the best. Still, the fight at Beecher Island was a vicious engagement.

The **Battle of Beecher Island site** is off County Road KK, seventeen miles south of Wray off US 385. A large stone obelisk on a granite base commemorating the battle was placed at the site in 1905 and rebuilt after a flood toppled it in 1935.

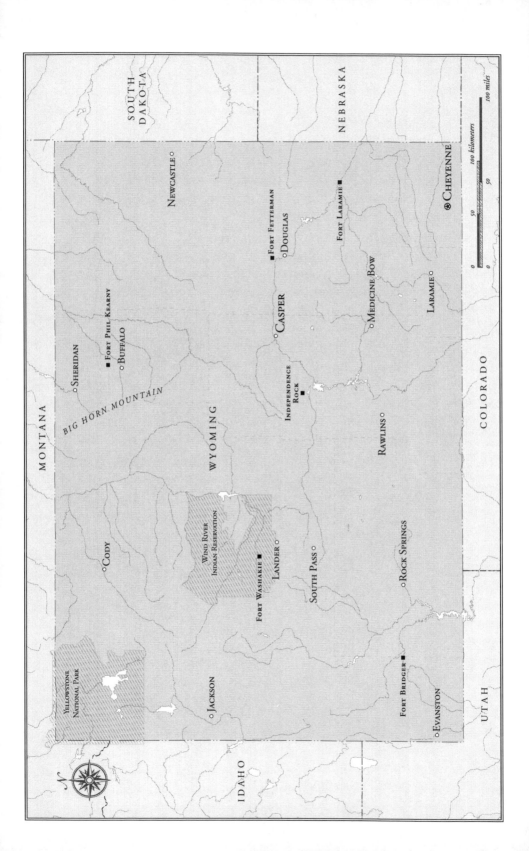

WYOMING

Baggs (Carbon County)

A small community in southern Wyoming just north of the Colorado state line, Baggs was named for Texas cattleman George Baggs, who in 1871 drove a herd of longhorns up from the Lone Star State and began ranching at this point along the Little Snake River. Later, Baggs was said to be a hangout for Butch Cassidy and the Wild Bunch.

Outlaws are no longer welcome, but the museum complex known as the **Outlaw Stop** (250 North Penland St./State Highway 789; 307-383-7262) is happy to have visitors. One of the museum's two buildings is the log Matthews-Gaddis House, an old roadhouse and dance hall owned by Ivy Pearl Mathews Gaddis for more than seven decades. Cassidy and his gang were occasional visitors, enjoying a meal and entertainment. The other building on the site is the combined old town hall, fire station, and jail. Cassidy never cooled his heels there, but other rough Western characters did.

Eleven and a half miles east of Baggs, the **Little Snake River Museum** (13 County Road 561 North, Savery; 307-383-7262) covers the history of the Little Snake River valley.

Buffalo (Johnson County)

After the Indian Wars on the Northern Plains ended, Buffalo was founded in 1879. Lying at the base of the Bighorn Mountains, the town became a commercial center for sheep raisers and cattlemen in the area.

Built in 1880 on the Bozeman Trail at the edge of the Bighorn Mountains, the Occidental (a commonly used nineteenth-century synonym for "western") became one of the West's most elegant and best-known accommodations. Famous folks who stayed at the hotel over the years include Buffalo Bill, Calamity Jane, Butch Cassidy, hired killer Tom Horn, and future president Theodore Roosevelt. Writer Owen Wister gave the hotel lasting literary life in his classic work *The Virginian: A Horseman of the Plains.* The 1902 novel's climactic gunfight is set in a hotel based on the Occidental. Despite all the time Wister spent in Wyoming, there's no record he ever stayed at the Occidental, but historians agree he knew of the hotel and likely had it in mind in writing his gunfight scene.

By the early 1980s, the Occidental's future did not look promising. The upstairs rooms had been closed and a portion of the downstairs accommodated the local bus depot. About the only thing keeping the place in business was the monthly rent paid by permanent residents. But in 1997 new owners, realizing the hotel's rich history would be an attraction, renovated it and reopened for overnight guests as the **Occidental Hotel** (10 North Main St.; 307-684-0451).

Fort Phil Kearny

The US Army occupied Fort Phil Kearny for only two years, from 1866 to 1868, but if not for the grit of one determined man, the post could have been the site of one of the Indian War's deadliest battles.

On December 21, 1866, in the frontier army's worst defeat at the hands of American Indians prior to George Armstrong Custer's 1876 debacle at Little Big Horn, Capt. William J. Fetterman and eighty of his troopers were killed to a man by a larger Sioux Indian war party under Chief Red Cloud. At nearby Fort Phil Kearny, post commander Col. Harry B. Carrington feared the Indians would soon attack the fort. Half his command had died with Fetterman, leaving too small a force to successfully defend the post. Desperately needing reinforcements, the colonel called for civilian volunteers willing to ride from the fort to request help from Fort Laramie, 236 miles to the south. Two men stepped up: John "Portuguese" Phillips and his friend Daniel Dixon. Whether Dixon died along the way or dropped out is not known, but four days later, Phillips made it. His horse died and Phillips nearly did, but within an hour of his arrival at Fort Laramie, troops departed to bolster Fort Phil Kearny's garrison.

Fort Phil Kearny State Historic Site is twelve miles north of Buffalo off I-90 at exit 44, Banner. Indians burned the fort to the ground after the army left, but the locations of buildings are marked. A visitor center (307-684-7629) has exhibits on the fort, the Fetterman Massacre, and other events connected to the conflict with Red Cloud.

In 1892 Buffalo became the focal point for one of the darker episodes in Wild West history—the **Johnson County War**. Ostensibly, the big cattlemen and their Wyoming Stock Grower's Association (so cozy with leading state officials that it headquartered in the state's capitol) were fighting to rid their ranges of cattle rustlers. But as one modern historian put it, in the case of this range war, the good guys were really the bad guys, and the bad guys were really the good guys. In actuality, the cattle barons and the new state's powerful politicians were trying to force out small homesteading operators by branding them as rustlers.

The conflict began as a series of assassinations of some of the "rustlers" and escalated into the wealthy cattle barons hiring a contingent of gunmen from Texas to serve as what amounted to a private army (soon called the Invaders) charged with driving the homesteaders from northern Wyoming.

On December 1, 1891, John A. Tisdale, one of the small-time cattlemen homesteading in the vicinity of Buffalo, was on his way home from a shopping trip into town—his wagon loaded with winter supplies and Christmas presents for his family—when someone shot him in the back. An unknown assassin also shot and killed Orley Jones around the same time, his body found after the discovery of Tisdale's. The murders, never solved, outraged Johnson County residents and lit the figurative fuse to the explosion of violence that followed.

A state historical marker stands on the east side of State Highway 196 six miles south of Buffalo near the Tisdale murder site at a point called the Tisdale Divide. A bronze statue of Johnson County War victim Nate Champion stands at the entrance of **Jim Gatchell Memorial**

Museum (100 Fort St.; 307-684-9331), which has numerous artifacts, documents, and photographs bearing on the war, including an Invader's rifle and the pistol and holster that belonged to Champion's associate Nick Ray. Ray died along with Champion in the April 9, 1892, Invader versus "rustlers" siege at Kaycee (see Kaycee, Wyoming).

The battle took place on what is now the **TA Guest Ranch** (28623 Old Highway 87; 307-684-5833). Defensive trenches dug by the two factions are still visible, as are bullet holes in ranch structures, an 1883 barn, and a ranch house. The ranch is near present Kaycee, thirteen miles south of Buffalo on State Highway 196. A state historical marker on the east side of the highway summarizes the TA Ranch fight.

Five men who figured in the Johnson County War are buried in Buffalo's **Willow Creek Cemetery** (351 North Adams Ave.; GPS coordinates: N44° 20.09', W106° 42.19'): Johnson County sheriff William "Red" Angus (1849–1920), block 4, section 18; dry gulch victim John Tisdale (1855–1891), block 2, section 4; Nathaniel Champion (1857–1892) and Nick Ray (1864–1892), block 9, section 7; and Joe LeFors (1865–1940), who extracted a murder confession from Tom Horn, block 51, section 8, space 1.

CASPER (NATRONA COUNTY)

Initially a trading post at a crossing of the North Platte River, the town got its start when the Fremont, Elkhorn and Missouri Valley Railroad came to Wyoming Territory in 1888, but long before then the area was a western crossroads. The new railroad stop came to be called Casper for a nearby abandoned military post, Fort Casper, a post already in ruins at the time. But by all rights, Casper, as well as the earlier military post, should have been Caspar. The US Army named the fort for Lt. Caspar Collins, killed by Indians with thirty-six of his men near the post in 1865. Early on, someone accidentally substituted an "e" for an "a" in honoring the fallen officer, and the mistake stuck. Beginning in 1888, the town saw some oil play, one of only a handful of wells drilled in the West during the nineteenth century. The real boom came early in the twentieth century, and now Casper bills itself as Oil City.

Founded in 2002, the **National Historic Trails Interpretive Center** (1501 North Poplar St.; 307-261-7700) focuses on the four pioneer routes that helped shape the West—the Oregon, California, and Mormon Trails, and the Pony Express route. Permanent and temporary exhibits tell the epic story. Part of Casper College, the **Western History Center** (125 College Dr.; 307-268-2680) has a large collection of primary source material on Wyoming and the West, with emphasis on Casper and Natrona County.

Independence Rock

Some travelers said it looked like a giant loaf of bread. Or a whale. Or half an apple. Descriptions varied, but when the large granite monolith loomed ahead, emigrants headed west on the Oregon Trail knew they were on schedule to reach their destination before snow began to fall if they got to this waypoint by the Fourth of July. Accordingly, it came to be called Independence Rock. Often travelers stayed here for a day or two to celebrate the young nation's independence from Great Britain and their good fortune in likely being able to dodge severe winter weather on their journey. Succumbing to a human characteristic that dates back long before their time, many of the travelers scratched their name on the rock.

Independence Rock, nearly 140 feet high and roughly a mile in circumference, stands near a roadside park off State Highway 220, fifty-five miles southwest of Casper. Interpretive signage relates the history of this once important waymark, now a Wyoming state historic site.

The army established an outpost called Platte River Station to protect the mail route and the first transcontinental telegraph line in 1862. Following an Oglala Sioux attack on a cavalry wagon train escort in 1865 that left twenty-six soldiers dead, the military upgraded the North Platte camp into **Fort Caspar.** The army abandoned the post in 1867 when the Union Pacific cut through southern Wyoming and the telegraph line was relocated along its tracks.

Little remained of the original fort, but in 1936 the federal Works Progress Administration built a replica. Signage at the reconstructed fort corrects the misspelling of its namesake's given name, but the nearby town is still Casper. Today the **Fort Caspar Historic Site** (4001 Fort Caspar Rd.; 307-235-8462) has a three-thousand-square-foot museum, a section of the one-thousand-yard wood bridge that once spanned the river, and reconstructed enlisted men's barracks, officer's quarters, a commissary, and a blacksmith's shop. Historic artifacts include period rifles such as an 1857 .50-caliber Smith carbine, an 1860 Spencer repeating carbine, and a Colt pistol.

Most victims of Wild West lynching were men, but occasionally a woman ended up at the end of a rope. Ellen L. Watson, better known as "Cattle Kate," and James Averell were hanged in Spring Canyon on July 20, 1889. Why that happened is related in two opposing narratives. The most prevalent story is that they were strung up for cattle rustling. The other version has them hanged because others wanted their well-watered land.

The lynching took place about fifty miles southwest of Casper near Independence Rock. The graves of Watson and Averill were covered when Pathfinder Reservoir filled in 1909, and the site of the hanging is on private property. But a historical marker placed by the Natrona County Historical Society outside the Fort Casper Museum, sets forth the two stories behind the double hanging.

What happened in Natrona County in the spring of 1890 was, as the *Wyoming Derrick* declared, "A Devil's Deed."

A man named Dogie (in some spellings Dogae) Lee ran one of Casper's nine rough-edged entertainment venues—a combination saloon, gambling joint, dance hall, and bawdy house. Lee's most popular prostitute was strikingly attractive twenty-three-year-old Louella Polk. Soon Lee saw her as more than his top money-maker—he was in love . . . or lust. Jealous that Louella seemed interested in another man, Lee lured her from town on the pretense of going for a horse-back ride. Instead, he kidnapped her at gunpoint, alternately saying he intended to take her far away and kill her, or fix her so that no man would ever again want her. The ordeal lasted several days before a rageful Lee threw her down, drew a knife, and slashed off her nose. Mutilated for life, Louella finally escaped her tormenter and made it back to town. With the sheriff already on his trail, Lee left that part of Wyoming and was never seen again.

Louella took possession of the dance hall and soon wore a carved wooden nose held in place by glasses. Even with that cosmetic improvement, she never appeared in public without a veil over her face. A few months later, Casper's first murder took place on September 20, 1890, in Louella's place when John C. Conway, a tough she employed as a bouncer, shot and killed a cowboy named John "Red Jack" Tidwell.

At first sympathetic toward her, in time the people of Casper decided they no longer wanted a woman of her type—or any of her competitors—doing business in their community. Forced out of town, Louella took up her trade in a Nevada mining town. In 1907, looking considerably older than her forty years and in failing health, she returned to Casper and died there that August 17.

A 1964 telling of Louella Polk's story noted that she had not been buried under her real name for fear that her final resting place might be desecrated. Old-timers, the author said, also tried to keep the whereabouts of the grave secret. While true that her tombstone bears another name, the marker's location is known. In the old section of **Highland Cemetery** (1860 East 12th St.; 307-235-8317) is a tall monument bearing only the inscription "Lulu 1867-1907" (block 6, lot 5, grave 1). At its base is chiseled the odd surname "Cocoran." Casper's first homicide victim, Tidwell, is buried in the same cemetery (block 17, lot 4, grave 1E).

CHEYENNE (LARAMIE COUNTY)

First known as the "Magic City of the Plains," Cheyenne owes its existence to Union Pacific chief engineer Grenville M. Dodge. He selected the site as a division point for the transcontinental rail line, then steadily moving west, and began platting the town July 4, 1867. The following day, the army established Fort D.A. Russell to protect the coming community as well as the railroad, which reached town that November. By that time, Cheyenne already had four thousand residents, only 10 percent of them women.

Soon the Magic City had another name, "Hell on Wheels." Its streets crowded with railroad men, soldiers, and new arrivals eager to cash in on the boom, violence became commonplace as the usual ensemble of saloons, gambling houses, and bordellos did a flourishing business. Miners and cattlemen added to the volatile mix. In the absence of traditional law enforcement, by January 1868 Cheyenne had an ever-alert vigilance committee. When someone killed a man other than in self-defense, that person was duly lynched. Just as the new town had no lawmen, Cheyenne had no trees. Despite that impediment to traditional lynching, resourceful vigilantes fashioned tripods from poles suitable for the suspension of undesirables. Cheyenne had legitimate law enforcement by 1870 and lynching decreased. Even so, the town's rowdy nature continued, with Sheriff Thomas Jefferson Carr conducting the state's first legal execution in 1871.

In the 1880s and on into the 1890s, substantial stone buildings began going up to replace the town's original wooden buildings. Some of its nineteenth-century architecture has been lost over the years, but Cheyenne still has scores of historic buildings and houses. The city has six historic districts, the downtown district alone having forty-two historic buildings.

The Cheyenne Downtown Development Authority distributes a sixty-eight-page booklet mapping three walking tours with historical summaries and locations for seventy-nine downtown historic sites, from the state capitol to where infamous bordellos once stood. The guide is available at the **Cheyenne Visitor Center** (121 West 15th; 307-778-3133).

In 1887, twenty years after the Union Pacific first reached Cheyenne, the railroad replaced its original frame depot with a large, two-color stone train station that still stands. Three years later a Seth Thomas clock that would still be keeping time well into the twenty-first century crowned the depot's distinctive tower. Restored in 2004, the **Union Pacific Depot** (121 West 15th St.; 307-632-3905) is a registered National Historic Landmark and houses a museum that tells the Union Pacific story.

The 1970 Western film *The Cheyenne Social Club*, pure fiction other than being set in Cheyenne, still made the Cheyenne Club famous. First called the Cactus Club, it was organized in 1880 as a private club for wealthy cattlemen. Never a bordello as portrayed in the movie, the club featured a fancy dining room offering gourmet meals, a billiard room, card rooms, a well-appointed bar-smoking lounge, and a reading room. Apartments on the second floor were available to members and guests. Under penalty of loss of membership, no gambling, drunkenness, fighting, or profanity was allowed. The killer blizzard of 1886–1887 ruined a lot of the cattle barons, and the club went into decline, but it continued as a cowboy hangout until 1909. After that, the building saw various uses until razed in 1936.

An interpretive plaque on a square stone base at 120 East 17th Street, placed by the Cheyenne Historic Preservation Board, relates the club's history. On the sidewalk around the marker, a bronze coyote is frozen in its pursuit of a long-eared jackrabbit, a piece of public art called *Fast Food*.

Especially in the relatively low-overhead free-range days before the advent of barbed wire, a lot of money could be made in the cattle business. Conversely, drought, severe winters, livestock disease, changing markets, and other factors could dry up profits faster than a thirsty herd crowding around a shallow water hole.

But when times were good, they were good. That's how 17th Street—lined with the Victorian-era mansions of wealthy cattlemen—became known as **Cattle Baron's Row.** In the East it would be called the city's silk-stocking district. In the West, custom-made boot district would be more apt.

Today more commonly referred to as the Rainsford District for George D. Rainsford, the architect who designed many of the houses, the area just east of downtown has dozens of historic structures, from cottages to mansions. Seventeenth Street alone has seventeen houses listed on the National Register of Historic Places. The walking tour guide available at the visitor center lists the more notable old houses on or around Cattle Baron's Row.

Tom Horn

While all the bloodshed associated with the 1892 Johnson County War happened elsewhere in Wyoming, many key players—especially on the cattle baron side—had connections to Cheyenne, either as their place of residence or where they officed. In addition, as the state capital, Cheyenne was home to elected officials, military officers, and federal lawmen. One of those lawmen was deputy US Marshal Joe LeFors, who played the lead role in closing the colorful career of Tom Horn.

On July 18, 1901, someone killed fourteen-year-old Willie Nickell at Iron Mountain, northwest of Cheyenne. Son of sheep rancher Kel Nickell, the teenager happened to be wearing his father's coat and riding his father's horse when shot by a hidden rifleman. The prevailing theory was that whoever shot young Nickell had killed him by mistake, intending instead to bushwhack his father. A range detective working for the Wyoming Cattlemen's Association, Horn came under suspicion, but there was nothing to tie him to the murder. Trying a different tack, LeFors, posing as a Montana rancher, got Horn talking by getting him drunk. Eventually Horn boasted of making the best shot he'd ever made in killing the boy. Unfortunately for Horn, LeFors had a stenographer hidden in an adjoining room taking down everything Horn said. It still wasn't the best of cases, and there's a reasonable argument that Horn didn't kill the boy, but his conversation with LeFors was enough to get Horn convicted and sentenced to hang.

LeFors's meeting with Horn took place in an office on the second floor of the Commercial Bank Building. The building still stands at 216-218 West 16th Street (Lincoln Way) in downtown Cheyenne. The office was behind a bay window that's still there.

Following his trial, Horn was hanged at the county jail on November 20, 1903. That structure was later torn down to make room for the present courthouse at 309 West 20th Street.

Founded in 1875 as City Cemetery and renamed **Lakeview Cemetery** (2501 Seymour Ave.; 307-637-6402) in 1932, it is Cheyenne's oldest cemetery. Among numerous notable permanent residents are John Coble (1859–1914), lot 1230, Coble family plot, a Tom Horn associate who killed himself in Elko, Nevada; James P. Julien (?–1932), lot 2101, section F, grave unmarked, the architect who designed the water-powered gallows used to hang Horn; John "Portuguese" Phillips (1832–1936), the messenger whose desperate ride saved Fort Phil Kearny in 1866; and Johnny Slaughter, a driver for the Deadwood Stage Line killed by robbers in 1877. A booklet available at the cemetery office guides visitors to twenty-two graves of historical personages, from former Wyoming governors to murder victim Willie Nickell (Nickell's grave is in lot 950, space D).

On July 18, 1901, someone killed fourteen-year-old Willie Nickell. Son of sheep rancher Kel Nickell, the teenager happened to be wearing his father's coat and riding his father's horse when shot by a hidden rifleman. The prevailing theory was that whoever shot young Nickell had killed him by mistake, intending instead to bushwhack his father. Tom Horn came under suspicion, but there was nothing to tie him to the murder. Trying a different tact, deputy US Marshal Joe LeFors, posing as a Montana rancher, got Horn talking by getting him drunk. Eventually Horn boasted of making the best shot he'd ever made in killing the boy. Unfortunately for Horn, LeFors had a stenographer hidden in an adjoining room taking down everything Horn said. It still wasn't the best of cases, but it was enough to get Horn convicted and sentenced to death.

Founded in 1895, only five years after Wyoming became a state, the **Wyoming State Historical Museum** (2301 Central Ave.; 307-777-7022) covers the state's history from the time of the dinosaurs, to the American Indians who once held all of what became Wyoming, to the Euro-Americans who settled it. Among the museum's many thousands of artifacts is a pair of Shoshone moccasins that belonged to Ella Watson, better known as "Cattle Kate" (see Casper, Wyoming).

Cheyenne started celebrating its frontier heritage in 1897 with a rodeo and other festivities, and it hasn't stopped. Now called Cheyenne Frontier Days, the annual July event—something of a Western-themed state fair—has continued to grow in scope and attendance. Opened in 1978 and operated by a nonprofit organization, **Cheyenne Frontier Days and Old West Museum** (4610 Carey Ave.; 307-778-7290) focuses on the event's history and the Old West in general. One of the highlights is a large collection of vintage horse-drawn vehicles.

Fine Western art, American Indian cultural material, and rodeo-cowboy objects make up the bulk of the **Nelson Museum of the American West's** (1714 Carey Ave.; 307-635-7670) fourteen-thousand-plus artifacts, but it also has a collection of mounted game animals, firearms, and objects related to the West's military and law enforcement history.

CODY (PARK COUNTY)

The citizens of Cody did not name their town in honor of Buffalo Bill—he did. In 1895, ready for a change after living for years in Nebraska, Cody bought land in Wyoming's Big Horn Basin and started a ranch. A year later he had a townsite surveyed along the Shoshone River. At first, he called it Cody City but soon dropped "City." His next enterprise involved digging a canal from the Shoshone River to allow for farming in the basin. In 1899, the new and still small town got a post office. The same year, the scout-turned-showman founded the town's first newspaper, the *Cody Enterprise*. In 1901 he convinced the Chicago, Burlington and Quincy Railroad to lay tracks to Cody. Finally, in 1902, on the build-it-and-they-will-come theory, he put up a thirty-six-room hotel he named after his daughter Irma.

Buffalo Bill once described his **Hotel Irma** (12th Street and Sheridan Avenue; 307-587-4221) as "just the sweetest hotel there ever was."

During his lifetime the Irma was not always the showplace he wanted it to be, but over the years it has accommodated Yellowstone-bound tourists, big game hunters, celebrities, ranchers, mine investors, and just plain folks. A 1929 addition gave the hotel more rooms, followed by another expansion and renovation in 1976. The noted hostelry is still doing business, along with its restaurant and bar. The centerpiece of that watering hole is a cherrywood bar given to Cody by Queen Victoria.

Problem was, at first no one came to Cody. The town did not gain traction as an investment until Cody convinced the government to start the first road to Yellowstone National Park in Cody. That happened in 1905. Tourists bound for Yellowstone drove the economy for years, but after Cody the man died in 1917, Cody the town began a new life. Not only did tourists still pass through on their way to the national park, but people began coming to Cody to learn more about the man who played such a big part in creating the mythical Wild West.

The West covers a lot of territory and with three-hundred-thousand-plus square feet, so does the **Buffalo Bill Center of the West** (720 Sheridan Ave.; 307-587-4771). Of course, the museum has not always been that large. It opened in 1927, three years after the dedication of the town's first commemoration of its namesake, *Buffalo Bill—The Scout*, a larger-than-life bronze statue of Cody on horseback with a rifle in hand. Nearby, the museum continued to expand and see an increasing number of visitors. In 2012 the property was extensively renovated and renamed the Buffalo Bill Center of the West. The facility has five major collections, each a museum in its own right: the Buffalo Bill Museum, the Cody Firearms Museum, the Plains Indian Museum, the Draper Museum of Natural History, and the Whitney Gallery of Western Art. The center also has a major archival collection, the McCracken Research Library.

Buffalo Bill didn't spend all his time as a performer and town builder. He liked to play poker, and on one occasion, when betting and raises built a particularly large pot, he and his fellow card players agreed that whoever raked in the chips on that hand would donate his winnings to a church. When Cody's friend George Beck won, he used the money to help build a small wood-frame house of worship that still stands—Christ Episcopal Church at 825 Simpson.

What Buffalo Bill didn't do for Cody the town, Wyoming archaeologist Bob Edgar (1939–2012) did. In 1967, Edgar started **Old Trail Town** (1831 Demaris Dr.; 307-587-5302), a collection of restored historic cabins and buildings moved in from other parts of the state. The town has twenty-five vintage structures, including two cabins associated with the Wild Bunch gang and the log cabin of Curly, a Crow Indian scout for Lt. Col. George Armstrong Custer. In addition to its structures, Old Trail Town is the final resting place of mountain man "Liver-Eating" Johnson (1824?–1900). The grave of the famous hunter, trapper, scout, soldier, and lawman (later portrayed by Robert Redford in the movie *Jeremiah Johnson*) was relocated to Old Trail Town in 1974. In 1981, a bronze statue of Johnson by Peter Fillerup was placed over his grave.

DOUGLAS (CONVERSE COUNTY)

Named for Senator Stephen A. Douglas, this town on the banks of the North Platte River began in the mid-1880s when the Wyoming Central Railway made it a train stop. But settlement in the area dates to 1867, with the establishment of nearby Fort Fetterman.

The **Fort Fetterman State Historic Site** (752 State Highway 93; 307-358-2864) was named for Capt. William J. Fetterman, who died along with all his command when led into an ambush by Sioux Indians under Red Cloud (see Buffalo, Wyoming). Two original buildings still stand along with a reconstructed officer's quarters and warehouse. The site is seven miles north of Douglas.

A contender for best legitimate epitaph in the West belongs to George W. Pike (1855–1908). It reads like one of Tombstone's phony grave markers made to appeal to tourists, but the words carved on Pike's headstone have been there since shortly after his death:

Underneath this stone in eternal rest
Sleeps the wildest one of the wayward west.

He was a gambler and sport and cowboy too
And he led the pace in an outlaw crew.
He was sure on the trigger and stayed to the end,
But he never was known to quit on a friend.
In the relations of death all mankind is alike,
But in life there was only one Geo. W. Pike.

Pike is buried in **Douglas Park Cemetery** (9th and Ash Streets; 307-358-3047). Douglas's Pioneer Museum (see below) has a self-guided cemetery tour pointing out notable burials.

One-time horse thief David C. "Doc" Middleton, whose real name was James M. Riley, did time in Nebraska but escaped twice. After the second breakout, he felt it prudent to change his name and became Doc Middleton. He turned to peddling whiskey as a saloonkeeper instead of selling stolen horses. Operating variously in Nebraska, South Dakota, and Wyoming, he died of pneumonia in Douglas on December 27, 1913. Middleton is also buried in Douglas Park Cemetery (section 3, block 2, lot 3, space 2).

Much Wild West history remained to be made when Wyoming pioneers first gathered in 1884 to talk about the good old days. The pioneers began meeting every year starting in 1905 during the state fair and incorporated in 1926. They defined a Wyoming pioneer as someone twenty-one or older who lived or did business in Wyoming Territory prior to July 1, 1884. Though the original pioneers are long gone, the association serves the **Pioneer Memorial Museum** (400 West Center St.; 307-358-9288) in an advisory capacity, while the state operates it. Located on the Wyoming State Fairgrounds, the museum has two floors of exhibits on the history of Wyoming and western expansion.

ENCAMPMENT (CARBON COUNTY)

Fur trappers, the first Euro-American Westerners other than government-funded explorers, met annually for what they called a rendezvous. In 1838, at a point in the upper end of the North Platte Valley, a group of trappers gathered at a spot they called Camp le

Grande. Trapping eventually declined when beaver-skin hats fell out of fashion back East, but the place name endured, albeit in English. When prospectors found copper in the vicinity in 1867, the mining town that developed there was called Grand Encampment. The copper played out in the early 1900s, and, Grand Encampment no longer being very grand, that part of its name was relegated to the cartographic slag heap.

Organized by deep-rooted local families, the **Grand Encampment Museum** (807 Barrett Ave.; 307-327-5308) focuses on the history of the upper North Platte. In addition to interpretive exhibits and artifacts, the museum preserves a collection of fifteen restored historic structures, including a two-story outhouse. Archival material held by the museum includes the Nora Webb Nichols collection of twenty-thousand-plus photographs taken in the early 1900s. The images document the everyday lives of Carbon County people, from families to miners, timbermen, and ranchers.

EVANSTON (UINTA COUNTY)

Evanston began as a rough-and-tumble railroad town when the Union Pacific put down tracks across southern Wyoming Territory in 1869. Excepting mining and an oil boom at the turn of the twentieth century, the town's mainstay has always been ranching.

The **Uinta County Museum** (1020 Front St.; 307-789-8248) has interpretive exhibits on the area's history, a saga it summarizes as one of "Trails, Rails, Ranches and Rigs." The **Chinese Joss House Museum** (10th and Front Streets; 307-783-6320) focuses on the Chinese rail workers who established a community in Evanston.

In 1842, mountain man Jim Bridger and partner Louis Vasquez opened a fur trading post along the Oregon Trail roughly midway between the route's starting point in Missouri and The Dalles in Oregon. They called the place **Fort Bridger.** The two men had sold out by 1853 and the Mormons used it for a time—and then burned it down—during the short-lived Mormon War. In 1858, the US Army built a new fort at the site and occupied it intermittently until 1890.

Fort Bridger became a Wyoming Historic Landmark in 1933. The site includes a reconstruction of the trading post and an original stone barrack from 1888. Two museums interpret the fort's history. Fort Bridger (307-782-3842) is thirty-four miles east of Evanston, three miles south of I-80, exit 34.

Bear River City Riot

Most of the western communities that became ghost towns died when their economic reason for being withered. But **Bear River City** essentially shot itself in the foot when a riot erupted November 19, 1868, between vigilantes and friends of a railroad worker that the self-appointed law-and-order group had just lynched. A sole lawman, town marshal Thomas J. Smith, valiantly tried to separate the two factions, but one peace officer could not control that many armed men. By the end of the day, sixteen men had been killed in what came to be known as the **Bear River City Riot.** Only the deployment of soldiers from Fort Bridger and a declaration of martial law ended the violence. The timber harvesting town slowly faded until fire destroyed it in 1900. A historical marker in a remote area ten miles west of Evanston tells Bear River City's story.

FORT LARAMIE (GOSHEN COUNTY)

Built of cottonwood logs by fur traders in 1834—the first business enterprise west of the Missouri River—a trading post known as Fort William (for co-founder William Sublette) lay twenty days' travel beyond Fort Kearny (established in 1846 prior to Wyoming's Fort Phil Kearny) in Nebraska and more than a month's trek away from Fort Bridger in southwestern Wyoming.

When the original trading post began to show its age in 1842, the American Fur Company replaced it with a larger adobe structure they named Fort John. The trading post being a major waypoint on the Oregon Trail, the US Army purchased it in 1849 and renamed it Fort Laramie. Given its strategic location at the confluence of the Laramie and North Platte Rivers, the fort grew to become the largest and best-known garrison on the Northern Plains before its abandonment in 1890.

Lumber and other reusable material from the fort's sixty buildings was sold at auction, and by the early twentieth century only thirteen original buildings and eleven ruins still stood. In 1937 the state bought 214 acres around the old fort and a year later conveyed it to the National Park Service, which preserves it as the **Fort Laramie National Historic Site** (965 Gray Rocks Rd.; 307-837-2221).

Eighteen miles west of Fort Laramie is the state-preserved Register Cliff historic site. The first night's camping spot on the Oregon Trail west of the military post was beneath a one-hundred-foot-tall limestone bluff. The place came to be called Register Cliff because of the hundreds of names carved into the rock by fur traders and, later, Pacific Coast–bound emigrants. The first recognizable date on the cliff is July 14, 1829. To reach the site, from the town of Guernsey (on US 26), take Guernsey Road southeast to a sign pointing to **Register Cliff State Historic Site.**

Southwest of Guernsey are the so-called Guernsey Ruts, the most impressive surviving segment of the Oregon Trail. Formed by the passage of thousands of iron-rimmed wagon wheels over sandstone, the ruts are preserved as part of Wyoming's **Oregon Trail Ruts State Historic Site**. Take Guernsey Road south from Guernsey. After crossing the North Platte River, turn right (west) on Lucinda Rollins Road and follow it to a road leading south that ends at the site. Signs lead to the two-hundred-acre state property.

GREEN RIVER (SWEETWATER COUNTY)

Green River, named for the robust stream that passes by it, was another child of the Union Pacific. Founded in 1869, the railroad town is where John Wesley Powell began his 1869 and 1871 explorations on the Green and Colorado Rivers. A railroad division point, Green River became the seat of Sweetwater County in 1872.

The Green River Downtown National Historic District has eleven historically significant structures. The **Sweetwater County Museum**

(3 East Flaming Gorge Way; 307-872-6435) focuses on the history of the city and county. **Expedition Island Park** (475 South 2nd St.) is where Powell began his explorations and is a National Historic Site.

JACKSON (TETON COUNTY)

Lying between the Teton Mountains and the Gros Ventres in far western Wyoming, this town is properly just Jackson, even though many non-locals think it's Jackson Hole. But there is a "hole" lot of difference between Jackson and Jackson Hole. Jackson Hole is the valley surrounding Jackson. Mountain men and fur trappers started referring to the valley as a hole because they had to make their way down steep slopes to get to it. The first homesteaders arrived in 1884, quickly learning the valley was not suited for crops but made good pastureland. Named in 1893 for the first Euro-American known to have wintered in the valley—beaver trapper David "Davy" Jackson— the town remained a ranching community until the 1920s. That's when some enterprising landowners began offering a Wild West experience to Yellowstone and Grand Teton National Park visitors, and the local dude ranching–tourism industry was born.

Founded in 1958, the **Jackson Hole Historical Society and Museum** (225 North Cache St.; 307-733-2414) covers eleven thousand years of human occupation in Jackson Hole, from Paleo people to the development of the two national parks that have come to define the area.

KAYCEE (JOHNSON COUNTY)

Named for the KC Ranch, this small town was not founded until 1900, but the KC Ranch was the scene of the April 9, 1892, attack by the Invaders (aka hired guns from Texas) that claimed the lives of Nate Champion and Nick Ray during the Johnson County War (see Buffalo, Wyoming).

Founded by volunteers in 1989, the **Hoofprints of the Past Museum** (344 Nolan Ave.; 307-738-2381) focuses on area culture, from American Indians to artifacts connected to the Johnson County

War (the site of the cabin besieged and burned by the Texans was excavated in 1997) to the outlaw era.

Hole-in-the-Wall refers to a steep, narrow trail over the red-rock wall that flanks the Hole-in-the-Wall Valley. The trail is the only way into the valley from the east. Still isolated in the twenty-first century and even more desolate in the nineteenth and early twentieth century, Hole-in-the-Wall was a popular outlaw hideout. Several dozen stock thieves as well as bank and train robbers periodically holed up in the Hole-in-the-Wall, camping in six cabins that once stood in the valley. The most famous denizens of the Hole-in-the-Wall were Butch Cassidy and his colleagues.

The hideout is thirty-five miles southwest of Kaycee on the fifty-seven-thousand-acre Willow Creek Ranch, still an active cattle operation. A rough road leads from the ranch headquarters to the site, where only foundation remnants of the old cabins remain. Near this location, a half-mile trail leads to the famed Hole-in-the-Wall trail. The ranch has an office in Kaycee, but to obtain access or accommodations, call 307-738-2223 or visit the ranch website at willowcreekranch.com.

LANDER (FREMONT COUNTY)

The discovery of gold in the mountains of southwestern Wyoming in the 1860s drew the first Euro-American settlers to this region, but it was the treaty establishing the Wind River Reservation for the Shoshone in 1863 (with huge reductions in size coming in 1868 and 1874) that led to the settlement of the nearby town of Lander in the 1870s. Named for Frederick W. Lander, an engineer who in 1857–1858 blazed a wagon trail from Fort Hall, Idaho, to South Pass (a collective term for two passes through the Continental Divide used by Oregon Trail emigrants and other travelers), the town was incorporated in 1890. When the Chicago and North Western Railroad made Lander the western terminus of its line in 1906, the town became known as the place "where the rails end and the trails begin."

Two museums in Lander are devoted to the history of the area: the **Fremont County Pioneer Museum** (1443 Main St.; 307-332-3330) and the **Museum of the American West** (1445 West Main St.; 307-332-8778). Founded in 1998, the museum's Pioneer Village includes ten restored or reconstructed area historic structures.

Fifteen miles northwest of Lander, on the 2.2-million-acre Wind River Reservation, the **Eastern Shoshone Tribal Cultural Center** (90 Ethete Rd., Fort Washakie; 307-332-3177) focuses on Shoshone history and culture with interpretive exhibits, artifacts, and tribal artwork. Visitors will learn about Sacagawea, the young Shoshone woman who accompanied the Lewis and Clark Expedition (which could not have succeeded without a guarantee of safe passage by the Shoshone) and Chief Washakie (1810–1900), principal chief of the Shoshone for sixty years.

The US Army stationed troops at the reservation in 1869. First known as Camp Augur, and then Camp Brown, the post was designated as **Fort Washakie** in 1878 in honor of the well-respected Shoshone headman. The army decommissioned the fort in 1909 and transferred its buildings to the Shoshone Indian Agency. The fort was one of only two US military installations named for an American Indian. Chief Washakie is buried in the old post cemetery (GPS coordinates: N43° 00.28', W108° 53.42'). A fourteen-foot-tall statue of the chief stands across the road from the cemetery. It is similar to the statue of Washakie in the National Statuary Hall in the US Capitol.

LARAMIE (ALBANY COUNTY)

Laramie got its start with the establishment of Fort John Buford (later renamed Fort Sanders) in 1866, but its real beginning came with completion of the Union Pacific Railroad, which reached that point on May 4, 1868. A year later Laramie became a division point for the UP. A once rough town with a colorful history, the word "Laramie" has become synonymous with the Wild West. More than a dozen films or television shows have either had "Laramie" in their title or were set in Laramie.

The **Laramie Visitor Center** (210 East Custer St.; 307-745-4195) offers eight different self-guided walking tours related to various aspects of Laramie history. Built in 1892, the **Ivinson Mansion** (603

Ivinson Ave.; 307-742-4448) houses the **Laramie Plains Museum.**
An early Laramie merchant who became a civic leader and philanthropist, the British-born Ivinson was one of the three-member
committee that selected the site for the Wyoming Territorial Prison.

Built in 1872, the **Wyoming Territorial Prison** (975 Snowy
Range Rd.; 307-745-3733) is the state's oldest stone building (two-
foot-thick limestone and sandstone) and the place where one of the
Wild West's more notorious outlaws did time—Butch Cassidy. The
fortress-like lockup had forty-two cells split between two wings. Each
cell held two prisoners, who slept on canvas hammocks.

Convict No. 187, listed in prison records as George "Butch" Cassidy,
arrived on July 16, 1894, and did two years at hard labor. Cassidy was
one of 1,063 men and women who spent time within the prison's walls.

The prison continued in operation until 1903 when inmates were
transported to the new prison one hundred miles farther west in Rawlins. After the convicts were gone, the University of Wyoming used
the property for its agricultural school. In 1991, the site was opened
as a state park. The prison has been restored to its 1889 appearance,
and with photographs and artifacts paints a stark picture of a frontier
penal system. There is a large exhibit devoted to Butch Cassidy and
the so-called Outlaw Trail.

When Laramie deputy marshal "Long Steve" Young (often incor-
rectly referred to as "Big Steve" Long) decided to get hitched, maybe
he figured it was time to settle down, start a family, and quit killing
people. But as it turned out, getting engaged was the worst mistake
of his life.

Young had not been a very peaceful peace officer. On October 22,
1867, when a fight broke out inside the bar he ran with Asa Moore
and Con Wagner and spilled into the street, he shot and killed five of
the rowdies. By the following year, counting the five-in-one incident,
Young was said to have killed thirteen men and considered good
for several other deaths. Despite his supposed legal authority (some
accounts don't mention him as a lawman), Young and his colleagues
were without question outlaws.

On October 18, 1868, Young ambushed and robbed prospector Rollie "Hard Luck" Harrison. When "Hard Luck" tried to defend himself, Young shot and mortally wounded him. Before he died, however, "Hard Luck" managed to wing Young.

The outlaw lawman went to his fiancée for succor. While she bandaged his wound, he told her how it had happened. As soon as she could, she reported the crime to a vigilance committee led by drugstore owner Nathaniel K. Boswell (later elected Albany County's first sheriff). Ten days later, a party of concerned citizens removed Young, Moore, and Wagner from their saloon and walked them to a nearby log cabin under construction. By leaning a long pine rafter against one of its walls, the delegation was able to pull "Long Steve" and his partners in crime off the ground.

Realizing his time was up, Young had one last request: Could he remove his boots first? "My mother always said I'd die with my boots on," he supposedly said moments before he and his two associates ran out of air and time. Someone photographed the three hanging bodies, an image that has been published many times. The following day, the committee lynched a fourth undesirable, "Big Ned" Wilson, this time from a telegraph pole.

Young's sweetheart supposedly became sentimental after his lynching and had a monument placed over his grave. Where the grave is today is not known. Young and company's Belle of the West Saloon stood at the northeast corner of South First Street and East Garfield Avenue, facing the railroad tracks.

Opened in 2003, **Wyoming's House for Historic Women** (307 2nd St.; 307-721-2919) focuses on Louisa Ann Gardner Swain, who on September 6, 1870, became the first woman in the world to cast a ballot under a law granting women the right to vote with full civil equality with men. That enfranchisement came under a law passed by the territorial legislature, the 1869 Wyoming Suffrage Act. Another half century passed before ratification of the 19th Amendment giving women everywhere in the US the right to vote. The museum also honors a dozen other notable Wyoming women.

LUSK (NIOBRARA COUNTY)

Cattleman and railroad developer Frank Stillman Lusk, whose ranches lay fifteen miles northwest of the Rawhide Buttes community, disliked having to make a thirty-mile round-trip to check his mail. Accordingly, in 1886 he decided to apply for a post office on land he owned. After filling out the application, he once again rode to the Rawhide Buttes post office and turned in the document so it could be forwarded to Washington, DC. In reviewing it, the Rawhide Buttes postmaster noted that Lusk had not proposed a name for the new post office, so he filled in the blank for him. His suggestion was "Lusk," which was fine with the Post Office Department.

Mother Featherlegs

Born and raised in the remote swamp country of Tensas Parish in northern Louisiana, by 1876 Charlotte Shepard had lost a husband (whether through death, divorce, or abandonment is anyone's guess) and her two sons, Tom and Bill. What happened to the boys is known—each ended up stretching a rope. Their mother was no angel herself.

Charlotte and her new partner, a hard case known as "Dangerous Dick" Davis, decided to head west to Wyoming Territory. There, in future Niobrara County, they built a dugout on a hilltop overlooking the heavily traveled Deadwood–Cheyenne stagecoach road. The couple ran a combination gambling house, saloon, and bordello. Charlotte was the madam, but she also entertained customers. Of course, no one knew her real name at the time.

With all the humanity headed to the Black Hills during the gold rush, the couple's rowdy roadhouse saw a lively business. Red-haired Charlotte was lively enough herself, not at all shy about publicly exposing her lace-trimmed red pantalettes. When some cowboy opined that she looked like a feather-legged chicken, folks took to calling her Mother Featherlegs.

In 1879, the wife of a neighboring rancher, lonely for a visit with another woman no matter her profession, paid a call and found Mother Featherlegs's body sprawled near a spring not far from the dugout. She had been shot in the back while filling a water pail. Meanwhile, "Dangerous Dick" had decamped. A few years later, about to be hanged in Louisiana for another murder, Davis confessed to killing Charlotte and taking all her money, about $1,500.

In time, traffic along the road dried up, and by the mid-twentieth century, Mother Featherlegs and her violent demise had been all but forgotten. But Jim Griffith, editor of the *Lusk Herald*, knew the story and led a movement to place a monument over her grave. Not so much because of who she had been, but to preserve the history of what happened.

First, however, the exact location of Mother Featherlegs's burial had to be determined. Fortunately, one old-timer knew precisely where the monument should go. In 1893, as a teenager, he and a friend had dug open the murdered madame's grave, pried off the lid of her pine casket, and after the image of the well-preserved woman's face and ample red hair burned itself into their memory, quickly re-covered the grave.

The red granite marker, five feet high and weighing some 3,500 pounds, was dedicated on May 14, 1964, as part of the seventy-fifth anniversary observance of the founding of the Cheyenne-Deadwood Stage Line. Donations collected that day in a way proved that Mother Featherlegs was an angel. The money enabled completion of a new church in nearby Jay Elm that had been under construction for years.

Conceived by the editor of Wyoming's oldest weekly newspaper to recognize a colorful Wild West practitioner of the world's oldest profession, the monument is believed to be the only one in the US dedicated to a prostitute. To reach the site, travel two miles west of Lusk on US 20, turn south on Silver Springs Road, and continue about 10 miles; the monument is on the east side of the road.

Located in the old National Guard armory, the **Stagecoach Museum** (322 South Main St.; 307-334-3444) has two floors of exhibits dedicated to area history, including a surviving stagecoach that once ran past Mother Featherlegs's place on the Deadwood, South Dakota, to Cheyenne route. Among the numerous artifacts on display are a pair of lacy red pantalettes, not to mention a preserved two-headed calf.

MEDICINE BOW (CARBON COUNTY)

Steam locomotives "drank" a lot of water, an undiminishing demand necessitating regular watering stations along rail lines. In 1868, the Union Pacific built a water stop along the Medicine Bow River that developed into the small town of Medicine Bow. The town never boomed but did make it into the twenty-first century still having a zip code—and a degree of literary fame.

Harvard-educated lawyer Owen Wister, author of the first Western novel, spent some time in Medicine Bow in 1885 and later recast some of his experiences in his classic *The Virginian*. The young attorney is said to have heard the line he made famous, "When you call me that, smile," while sweating a poker game in Medicine Bow during which someone called deputy sheriff James Davis an SOB and he replied with those six words.

Seven years after publication of the ground-breaking novel, which drew heavily from Wister's experiences in Medicine Bow and elsewhere in Wyoming, construction began on a three-story hotel in 1909. The writer never spent the night here, but the **Virginian Hotel** (404 Lincoln Highway; 307-379-2377) was named after the classic book. However, the hotel does have exhibits bearing on Wister's life, and displays a page from one of his original manuscripts.

As a Bicentennial project the local Lion's Club moved a cabin Wister had used as a hunting lodge in the Jackson Hole area to Medicine Bow. The restored log cabin stands adjacent to the **Medicine Bow Museum** (405 Lincoln Highway; 307-379-2383), near the Owen Wister monument erected in 1939. The museum is housed in the 1913 railroad depot, built after a fire destroyed the original depot that Wister would have known.

MEETEETSE (PARK COUNTY)

Founded on the Greybull River in the 1890s, Meeteetse (a Shoshone word for "meeting place") was and is a cow town. Cowboys from the nearby Pitchfork Ranch, the first spread in the Big Horn Basin, kept things lively.

Meeteetse has only a few hundred residents, but three museums: the **Charles Belden Museum of Western Photography,** the **Meeteetse Museum,** and the **First National Bank Museum.** All are part of the Meeteetse museum district (247 State St.; 307-868-2423). Belden's photographs document life on the Pitchfork Ranch from 1914 to 1940.

NEWCASTLE (WESTON COUNTY)

With the approach of the Chicago, Burlington and Quincy Railroad in 1889, a subsidiary of the railroad chartered as the Lincoln Land Company sold lots for a new town on the line. The railroad also laid a seven-mile spur from Newcastle to the new coal mining town of Cambria. Both communities became rowdy boomtowns. Newcastle alone had fourteen saloons, along with gambling dens and houses of prostitution. Hoping to calm things down, the first ordinance adopted by Newcastle's town council prohibited the discharge of firearms.

At one point during the Ghost Dance troubles in 1890, a panicky citizenry stockpiled ammunition and hastily fortified the town's sturdiest building against possible Indian attack. Townspeople stacked sacks of flour in the windows hoping they'd stop bullets, but the effort proved to be an overabundance of caution. No hostiles appeared, and the flour went into biscuits and baked goods as intended.

Built in 1889 to house the Kilpatrick Brothers and Collins Commissary, the two-story brick building later became the **Antlers Hotel** (205 West Main St.) and still stands. The **Anna Miller Museum** (401 Delaware Ave.; 307-746-4188) has exhibits on the history of Newcastle, Cambria, and Weston County.

The Sheriff and the House of Blazes

Texas-born lawman John Owens (1843–1927) may not have had the twenty notches on his gun that some writers claimed, but he had dispatched at least two men while on the job. Well-liked, he took his duty as a peace officer seriously, but he viewed gambling laws as an intrusion on a man's right to lose or make money on the luck of the draw, the spin of the wheel, or the roll of the dice. Nor did he see prostitution as sinful or illegal.

Owens served briefly during the Civil War, but in 1863 he took a job as a scout on a wagon train to Fort Laramie, Wyoming. Later he scouted for the US Army, helped track outlaws, and ranched. In 1887 he worked as a special deputy at Lusk, but when Newcastle boomed as a coal mining town he moved there and built a combination gambling and dance hall called the House of Blazes. In 1892 he got elected county sheriff. Seeing no conflict of interest in running his establishment and enforcing the law, he kept the lamps burning at his House of Blazes.

His first wife died, he parted ways with a second, and by 1880 was married to Serena Bolt, an attractive dance hall girl. Though virtue had not been her long suit, she didn't like Owens's gambling and they divorced. In 1894 he married a fourth time at fifty-one years old and stayed with that woman until her death in 1906.

Owens continued to serve as sheriff until finally losing an election in 1910. Later, as a night watchman in Cambria, he killed a couple of would-be thieves, but charges against him didn't stick. Owens's last job was guarding convicts during construction of the State Industrial Institute at Worland. Visiting Thermopolis one day, he ran into ex-wife Serena. They decided to remarry and lived in Worland until he retired at seventy-eight in 1920. After that, they went back to Thermopolis and stayed together until he died on August 11, 1927, his eighty-fourth birthday.

Owens is buried in **Greenwood Cemetery,** near the intersection of Delaware Avenue and South Spokane Avenue. Entrance to the cemetery is a left turn off Delaware (to the west) when driving north on Delaware.

Pinedale (Sublette County)

This western Wyoming town was established in 1904 by John F. Patterson, who offered to operate a general store if the owners of two of the larger ranches in the Green River Valley agreed to donate five acres each for a townsite along Pine Creek. Ranchers Charles A. Peterson and Robert O. Graham liked the idea of having a well-stocked store handy and agreed to the deal. In addition to being a ranching center, Pinedale for a time was a supply point for tie hacks, men who made a living cutting timber and converting the logs into railroad ties.

Long before Pinedale was settled, the area was frequented by mountain men who from roughly 1820 to 1840 trapped beaver along streams across much of the Mountain West to supply the men's fashion rage of the day—beaver-pelt hats. A mountain man could do quite well in this business, but he had to be tough enough to deal with three serious impediments to success: Indians, grizzly bears, and weather. Those trappers who managed to stay alive from season to season met annually every summer to trade the pelts they had harvested during the winter for foodstuffs, clothing, guns, ammunition, and other vital supplies. These often-rowdy gatherings were called rendezvous, and while the word "rendezvous" was not new as a noun or verb, the mountain man meet-ups added to the definition.

The **Museum of the Mountain Man** (700 East Hennick; 307-367-4101) covers more than mountain men. While the mountain men certainly were the first Euro-Americans in the West, the museum also explores Plains Indian culture, the Oregon Trail, and other aspects of the region's history. The museum's permanent collection includes a .40-caliber rifle given to famed mountain man Jim Bridger by his business partner, Louis Vasquez, in 1853. To counterbalance that weapon, the museum displays a formidable Shoshone arm—a short bow made from a sheep's horn. A prized Shoshone possession, a sheep's horn bow was stronger (and therefore sent arrows traveling with a higher velocity) than bows made of wood.

RAWLINS (CARBON COUNTY)

After skirting north of the Medicine Bow Mountains, the 1867 surveying party laying out the route for the coming Union Pacific Railroad reached the flat, dry country called the Great Basin. Led by UP chief engineer Grenville Dodge, the entourage included his old friend General John A. Rawlins. The general suffered from tuberculosis and had joined Dodge on the expedition hoping the dry climate would improve his health. When a scout discovered a robust spring in what would become Carbon County, a thirsty Rawlins expressed his appreciation. "We will name this Rawlins Spring," Dodge is said to have declared. Rawlins went on to become Secretary of War under President Ulysses S. Grant, but the trip west had not helped, and he died in 1868. But the town that developed when the UP's tracks reached Rawlins Spring took his name. (At some point, "Spring" was dropped.) The town became a railroad division point with maintenance shops and other facilities, and later was selected as the site of the Wyoming Territorial Prison, both factors assuring its future.

In 1886 the Wyoming territorial legislature voted to move the territory's prison from Laramie to Rawlins. The cornerstone was laid in 1888, but funding issues delayed completion until 1901, eleven years after Wyoming had become a state. The stone, castle-like prison had its first inmates by 1902 and continued in use until the state opened a new prison in 1981. The old facility is home to the **Wyoming Frontier Prison Museum** (500 West Walnut; 307-324-4422).

The **Rawlins-Carbon County Chamber of Commerce** (509 West Cedar St.; 307-324-4111) has a self-guided walking tour of Rawlins's downtown National Historic District and material on other historic sites and attractions.

George Parrot Had Quite a Beak

In death, George Parrot realized a bizarre measure of immortality, though he would have just as soon kept on living, particularly if he wasn't behind bars. Better known as "Big Nose" George for reasons obvious to anyone seeing his photograph, Parrot and fellow outlaws decided to rob a Union Pacific train near Carbon, Wyoming, in August 1878. They flubbed an attempt to derail the train and hightailed it to Rattlesnake Pass, near Elk Mountain. Lawmen trailed them to their hideout, but the outlaws saw them coming and shot and killed two of them. After that, the gang scattered.

Two years later, in Montana, someone heard Parrot bragging about killing two peace officers in Wyoming. Local authorities arrested him and handed him over to Carbon County. Duly convicted of murder, Parrot was sentenced to hang on April 2, 1881. But on March 22 he made an unsuccessful escape attempt. Just as a precaution against him making another attempt at freedom, a mob removed him from jail and lynched him.

Dr. John Osborne pronounced Parrot dead. With a nod to posterity, the physician made a plaster death mask of the outlaw. While he was at it, he removed the skin from Parrot's chest and thighs, and had it tanned. Then he had a pair of shoes made from the human leather. No matter the doctor's eccentric souvenir collecting, Wyoming voters later elected him as governor.

With some thirty thousand artifacts and both permanent and changing exhibits, the **Carbon County Museum** (904 West Walnut St.; 307-328-2740) occupies a former church. "Big Nose" George's death mask, an ashtray made from his lower cranium, and Dr. Osborne's custom-made shoes are on display.

ROCK SPRINGS (SWEETWATER COUNTY)

Led by mountain man and scout Jim Bridger, in 1850 a military survey party under Capt. Howard Stansbury made a discovery that was only academic at the time: "We found a bed of bituminous coal cropping out of the north bluff of the valley, with every indication of its being quite abundant," the officer reported. At the time, at least on the Northern Plains, dried buffalo dung was more useful as a fuel than coal. But that changed in 1868 when the Union Pacific Railroad was building tracks through the area on its way west. Coal fired the boilers of steam locomotives.

A former Pony Express station named for Rock Spring, a nearby water source, became the site of a Union Pacific mining camp when the company began extracting coal from the nearby hills. From then until diesel engines ended the railroad's need for coal, Rock Springs was a coal mining boomtown with an international flavor. Its miners represented more than fifty countries, including China. Racial tension ignited a riot on September 2, 1882, that claimed twenty-eight Chinese lives. It took federal troops to suppress the violence.

The **Rock Springs Historical Museum** (201 B St.; 307-362-3138) offers a self-guided walking tour of Rock Springs' downtown historic district. The museum is housed in the former city hall, built in 1893 and restored in 1991, and has a display on Butch Cassidy.

Still pale from two years in the Wyoming State Prison, a thirty-year-old ex-con who called himself George Cassidy moved to Rock Springs in 1896. He could have gotten a job as a coal miner, but he had no interest in that. Cassidy landed a job at William "Walt" Gottsche's butcher shop. There, transforming cattle and hog carcasses into beef or pork, he picked up a nickname—"Butch." When not working, Cassidy is said to have frequented a saloon called the Fountain Club.

Long after his death in Bolivia in 1908, the legend prevailed in Rock Springs that Cassidy had survived that encounter in South America and occasionally slipped back into Sweetwater County to visit old friends and family. One of those family members was his sister, Lula Parker Betensen, who made the claim in her book, *Butch Cassidy, My Brother*.

The butcher shop stood at 432 Front Street. It is no longer there, but the old Fountain Club (514 South Main St.) still is, though not occupied and in need of renovation. Built in the 1880s, it is Rock Springs' oldest wood-frame structure.

Sheridan (Sheridan County)

Just east of the Bighorn Mountains, a fur trapper named Jim Mason built a cabin in 1878 that amounted to Sheridan's first structure. Three years later a new owner, Harry Mandel, repurposed the cabin as a general store and post office, naming the nascent community after himself. In 1882, the property changed hands again. This time new owner J.D. Loucks laid out a forty-acre townsite for a town he named after General Philip Sheridan. Primarily a ranching center, once it gained a rail connection in 1892, Sheridan benefited from coal mining in the area.

The **Sheridan Visitor Center and Museum** (1514 State Highway 336/5th St.; 307-673-7120) has exhibits focusing on the area's history and wildlife. The **Museum at the Bighorns** (850 Sibley Circle; 307-675-1150), formerly the Sheridan County Historical Society, focuses on the history of Sheridan, the county, and the nearby mountain range. The museum's most popular exhibit, "Crazy Horse, Crook, and the Battle of Rosebud Creek," tells the story of the June 17, 1876, battle that took place just eight days before Custer's defeat at the Little Bighorn.

Buffalo Bill Cody wasn't just a former scout and buffalo hunter turned showman. He also was a businessman. In 1894 his W.F. Cody Hotel Company began management of a newly built wood-frame, three-story, multi-gabled accommodation called the **Sheridan Inn** (856 Broadway; 307-674-2178). Cody stayed there on occasion and sometimes, to the delight of guests and passing train passengers, auditioned prospective Wild West show performers there. After Cody got out of the hotel business in 1896, the place saw a variety of owners, and in the 1960s was in danger of demolition when yet another owner took it over and renovated it. The twenty-two-room hotel remains open.

A good rope was essential in the Wild West, useful for everything from corralling a horse to hanging an undesirable—and except for hanging people ropes remain a basic tool. Started by Don King (1923–2007) in 1946 and still operated by his family, the **Don King's**

Saddlery and King Ropes (184 North Main St.; 307-672-2702) manufactures saddles and ropes. In addition to their retail business, they have a Western museum showcasing a wide range of artifacts and Western art.

SOUTH PASS CITY (CARTER COUNTY)

A prospector from Georgia supposedly found gold at the head of the Sweetwater River, but Indians killed him before he had a chance to profit from his discovery. However, no one knew for sure if he had really found gold or if it was only a rumor. A group of prospectors ventured into the area again in 1855, and while they survived the experience, Indians ran them off.

J.W. Lawrence finally found the vein, which came to be called the Carissa Lode, on June 8, 1867. While the presence of gold in the vicinity had been confirmed, Lawrence was also killed by Indians. Despite the danger, miners flocked to the area, and soon dozens of mines had been established, with a wide variety of names, from Miner's Delight to one honoring Texas called the Lone Star State Mine.

By 1870, the population was four thousand and Main Street extended a half mile. South Pass had a weekly newspaper, a bank, a city band, two breweries, three meat markets, three houses of prostitution, four lawyers, five hotels, six general stores, nine eateries, twelve saloons, and a combination bowling alley and shooting gallery. But the rich veins petered out, and by December 1873, South Pass had been deserted and the county seat of Carter County was moved to Green River.

South Pass City became a state historic site in 1969. The park features seventeen restored original buildings with more than thirty thousand artifacts on display (125 South Pass Main St.; 307-332-3684).

SUNDANCE (CROOK COUNTY)

Named for nearby Sundance Mountain, the town was founded in 1879. With a stagecoach line connecting Spearfish, South Dakota, with Sundance, the town grew as a commercial center for area ranchers. Later it became the county seat, a development that would give Sundance its biggest claim to fame.

Early in 1887, twenty-year-old Harry Alonzo Longabaugh began an eighteen-month sentence in the Crook County jail for stealing a horse. After doing his time, Longabaugh hooked up with Robert LeRoy Parker. Neither was interested in earning an honest living. Colleagues in crime, soon the pair became far better known as Butch Cassidy and the Sundance Kid.

The jail where Longabaugh served his sentence stood until 1972 when the county had it razed to make room for a new courthouse. The **Crook County Museum** (309 East Cleveland St.; 307-283-3666) displays the original court documents regarding the Kid's case and furniture from the courthouse where he was tried. Outside the museum, in a not-universally popular move, in 2004 the Sundance Area Chamber of Commerce dedicated a bronze statue of the Sundance Kid sitting jauntily in his jail cell, complete with his famous derby hat.

THERMOPOLIS (HOT SPRINGS COUNTY)

American Indians usually fought to keep their land, but those of the Northern Plains, particularly the Shoshone and Arapaho, saw the hot mineral springs in the vicinity of present Thermopolis as belonging to all. In 1896, the two tribes ceded the springs to the state government, calling it a "gift of the water." The tribes' only stipulation was that the springs be available at no charge to all people.

The state honored its commitment to allow free public use of the springs the tribes conveyed. The town, its name a combination of the Greek words for "heat" and "city," was founded in 1897 and, thanks to the gift from the Shoshone and Arapaho, developed as a resort.

At the Wyoming State Bath House in **Hot Springs State Park** (220 North Park St.; 307-864-2176), visitors can enjoy the 104-degree waters inside or outside the facility. Also part of the park, but not suitable for soaking, is the 127-degree Big Spring.

Operated by the county historical society, the **Hot Springs County Museum and Cultural Center** (700 Broadway; 307-864-5183) has two floors of exhibits on the county's history. The most popular attraction is the Hole in the Wall Bar, a re-creation of the saloon former Texas cattleman Tom Skinner built in Thermopolis, including the saloon's fancy cherrywood bar, imported from Ireland. Local lore has it that Butch Cassidy and the Sundance Kid frequented the bar. Historians say that's possible, but there is no documentation.

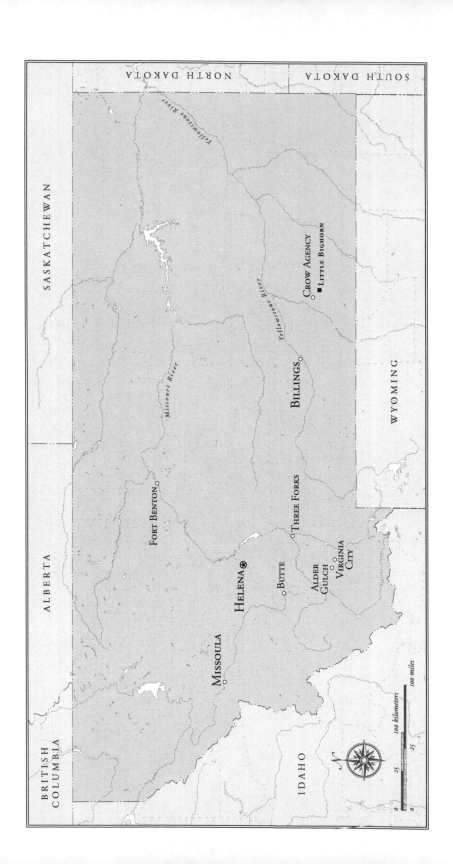

MONTANA

Bannack (Beaverhead County)

Prospectors from Colorado found gold along Grasshopper Creek in July 1862. Within weeks the mining camp that sprang up along the creek had four hundred residents, and Montana (then part of Washington Territory) had its first big gold rush, a half-million dollars in ore freighted from there by the end of the year. As soon as any of the miners took some time to think about it, they decided to call the camp-cum-town Bannock, for the Bannock Indians. But when the government opened a post office there in 1863, a year before the creation of Montana Territory, some bureaucrat mistakenly replaced the "o" for an "a" and Bannock became Bannack. No one ever bothered to correct the error.

3-7-77 Was an Unlucky Number for Outlaws

Because of the saloons and bawdy houses attendant to all Wild West boomtowns, the next thing Bannack needed after a post office was law enforcement. There being no traditional government, the miners appointed a man to serve as "sheriff." After that man resigned, the second so-called miner's sheriff was a man named Henry Plummer, appointed after a miner's court acquitted him of a barroom killing after concluding it happened in self-defense.

It would seem logical that with a dedicated law-and-order man on the job, even if he had no official legal standing, crime in the area would decrease. But the opposite happened. People traveling the fifty-two miles between Bannack and the nearby boomtown of Virginia City were frequently robbed, and some were getting killed. Plummer seemed unable to find the highwaymen.

But a group of concerned citizens who had pledged the restoration of law and order in their communities were having better luck. After barely a month in action, the vigilantes apprehended,

extra-legally convicted, and hanged twenty-four outlaws. Before
one of them received his "suspended sentence," he spilled the
proverbial beans. The gang's leader was Sheriff Plummer, who,
as it turned out, less than four years earlier had been doing time
in California's San Quentin Prison. Soon Plummer and two of
his deputies (aka gang members) dangled from the gallows that
Plummer had built to accommodate a miner's court hanging.

Long-standing legend holds that the vigilantes would paint
the numbers 3-7-77 on the doors of undesirables to suggest they
leave the area or else. The numbers represented the dimension of
a grave: 3 feet wide, 7 feet long, 77 inches deep.

A year later, Bannack had ten times as many residents as it had
started with. The man appointed as chief justice for the newly organized Idaho Territory (cut from Washington Territory) traveled to the
capital in Washington to push for creation of Montana Territory. The
effort proved successful. He became the new territory's first governor
and Bannack its first capital.

Everything seemed to be going Bannack's way except the town's
reason for being. The gold began to play out. In December 1864 the
new territorial legislature voted to move the seat of government to
Virginia City, and as ore production continued to decrease, Bannack
began slowly flowing down the sluice toward ghost town status. Still,
it took the community a long time to die. Not until the early 1940s
was the town finally abandoned.

The slow death proved a good thing for historical preservationists.
The old town remained mostly intact, and by 1954 the State of Montana acquired it for development as a state park. Some sixty historic
buildings, from the former county courthouse and later hotel to the
first two jails in Montana, have survived.

Bannack is twenty-five miles west of Dillon via I-15 to State
Highway 278 to its junction with Bannack Bench Road. The state
park is 3.7 miles south from that point. A replica of the gallows
(4200 Bannack Rd.; 406-834-3413) where Sheriff Plummer and his

accomplices were executed stands on the site of the original gallows. A three-foot piece from the original one is displayed at the **Beaverhead County Museum** (15 South Montana St., Dillon; 406-683-5027). The Montana Historical Society in Helena holds a shotgun that belonged to Plummer.

BIG TIMBER (SWEET GRASS COUNTY)

Big Timber, named for the giant cottonwood trees along the Yellowstone River, is a ranching community settled in 1882 when the Northern Pacific Railroad came through. The Lewis and Clark Expedition passed just north of the future town at a point they called "Rivers Across" because two streams flow into the Yellowstone there.

Towering northwest of Big Timber are the Crazy Mountains. Since inanimate objects are not capable of being crazy, how did the mountains get their name? Trying to discern that is enough to drive a person crazy, but the most common of numerous legends has to do with a family of westbound travelers supposedly attacked by American Indians. The only survivor, according to the tale, was the woman whose husband and children were killed. Having defended herself with an axe and slain some of the Indians, she is said to have lost her sanity, wandering in the mountains for the rest of her (short) life.

The **Crazy Mountain Museum** (2 South I-90 Frontage Rd.; 406-932-5126) covers the geology, archaeology, and pioneer history of Sweet Grass County and the nearby Crazy Mountains. One highlight is a twelve-by-six-foot miniature re-creation of Big Timber as it looked the year before a devastating fire in 1908 that charred a third of the town.

BILLINGS (YELLOWSTONE COUNTY)

Montana's largest city, Billings began with the appearance on open land of two parallel steel rails, the Northern Pacific Railroad. With track layers working west along the Yellowstone River, a group of investors organized the Minnesota & Montana Land & Improvement Company and in early 1882 surveyed a townsite they named for Frederick Billings, a former Northern Pacific president. Within a year more than a thousand people lived in Billings, earning it the nickname "The Magic City." (Billings wasn't the only Magic City in the Wild West, but it was the only one in Montana.) What came to be called the "Big Die-Up," an unusually severe cattle-killing winter in 1886–87, and an extensive fire made Billings a little less magical for a while, but the town grew as a livestock shipping point and commercial center.

The **Billings Visitor Center** (815 South 27th St.; 406-245-2635) offers maps and themed visitor guides. The **Yellowstone County Museum** (1950 Terminal Circle; 406-256-6811) occupies an 1892 log cabin on high ground overlooking Billings and the Yellowstone River valley near Logan International Airport. Its holdings include Northern Plains tribe artifacts, trapping equipment, and collections bearing on ranching and mining. The five-thousand-square-foot museum was founded in 1953 and has more than twenty thousand artifacts.

Located in the old Parmly Memorial Library (built in 1901, expanded in 1923, and used until 1969), the **Western Heritage Center** (2822 Montana Ave.; 406-256-6809) covers all phases of the Yellowstone River valley's history and culture. The building was named for Frederick Billings Sr.'s son Parmly and funded by Frederick Billings Jr. and his sister. A statue of the city's namesake stands at the northwest corner of the building. From American Indian beadwork to firearms to vintage photographs, the regional museum curates more than thirty-five thousand artifacts.

"I feel my body will rest better in Montana"

His legal name was Luther Sage Kelly, but he became much better known as Yellowstone Kelly. Born in 1849 in New York to a prosperous family and well-educated, he longed for a much larger classroom, the Wild West. Lying about his age, at sixteen years old he enlisted in the army in 1865 and was stationed in Dakota Territory. After his four-year enlistment ended, he began wandering the West, particularly along the Yellowstone River in Montana Territory. He trapped, hunted bears and other big game, traded, and served as an army scout and guide. During the Nez Perce War, he helped track down Chief Joseph.

Variously an explorer, rancher, Indian agent, soldier (again), and government worker, Kelly traveled extensively, from New York to California to Alaska and the Philippines. But it was the time he spent in the West that made him want to stay there forever. "I feel my body will rest better in Montana," he declared, "the scene of my earlier activities, than it would in the vastness of Arlington [National Cemetery]." When he died in 1928, two years after publishing his colorful memoir, his wish was granted, and he was buried on the rimrock above Billings.

The concrete slab that covered Kelly's grave was intended to be the base of a large monument in his honor, but it was never erected. In 1948 the army placed a bronze plaque over his grave. A few years later, the grave was vandalized; it was desecrated a second time in 2014. In 2015 a citizen's committee began work to restore the grave and develop an interpretive area at the site, which opened in 2017.

The **Yellowstone Kelly Interpretive Site** is in Swords Rimrock Park, just east of the airport; turn south from Airport Road on Black Otter Trail to the park. The grave and interpretive site is along a trail about a mile from the park entrance. Buried nearby is Crow Indian chief Black Otter, killed by a Sioux war party in 1861.

Like other western towns, Billings had its Boot Hill. But the **Boot Hill Cemetery** predates Billings, having been the burial ground for the earlier town of Coulson. Estimates on the number buried here range from twenty-plus to one hundred, with the last burial in 1887. One of the graves belongs to H.M. "Muggins" Taylor (1830–1882), a lawman shot to death in Coulson while trying to prevent the operator of a Chinese laundry from beating his wife. In 1876, as an army scout, he brought the first word of Custer's defeat to Bozeman after a 180-mile ride through Indian country. L.D. O'Donnell, a prominent Billings businessman with an interest in history, placed a marble monument at the cemetery in 1921. Inscribed on the obelisk is a short poem: "In memory of those who blazed the trail and showed to us our West/In boots and spurs they lie and on this hill find rest." The cemetery is located at the east end of the Rimrocks on a hill about a mile north of Coulson Park. It sits on a small rise southwest of the intersection of Main Street and Airport Road.

On July 25, 1806, the Lewis and Clark Expedition came to a 120-foot-high monolith at a point roughly halfway between future Billings and Miles City. William Clark named it Pompy's Tower for the seventeen-month-old son of the party's interpreter, Sacagawea. Having named the distinctive sandstone landmark, he felt the timeless urge to carve his name into the rock, the only known bit of graffiti connected to the expedition. By 1814, "Pillar" had replaced "Tower" in the landmark's name, but Clark's nineteenth-century version of "Kilroy was here" has endured. Since 1992, the signature has been protected as a National Historic Landmark. Nine years later the fifty-one-acre property became **Pompeys Pillar National Monument** (3039 US 312, Pompeys Pillar; 406-896-5013).

Chief Plenty Coups State Park

As a young man Aleek-Chea-Ahoosh (Plenty Coups) had a vision. He saw himself as an old man sitting beneath shade trees near a nice house. In time, as the last traditional chief of the Crow Nation, Plenty Coups acquired land on the Crow Indian Reservation and in 1884 built a log cabin that he eventually expanded into a two-story residence with gabled dormer windows and a covered porch. He farmed his land as long as he was able, planting cottonwoods and apple trees. His vision had come true. Realizing his life was nearing its end, in 1928 the chief and his wife Strikes the Iron gave 189 acres to Big Horn County for use as a park "as a token of my friendship for all people, both red and white." When the chief died in 1932, he was buried on the property. The state acquired the land in 1961, and it was opened as a state park five years later. In the early 1970s, the state added a museum and visitor center. **Chief Plenty Coups State Park** (1 Edgar/Pryor Rd., Pryor; 406-252-1289) is thirty-five miles south of Billings, one mile west of the small town of Pryor.

BOZEMAN (GALLATIN COUNTY)

The story of Bozeman's namesake is decidedly more interesting than the early history of Bozeman the town. As a former mayor later put it, "From the first its growth has been slow, but in many respects healthy and strong. It has never been what might be called a 'hurrah' town [and] never passed through an exciting or fictitious boom."

John N. Bozeman left his wife and children in Georgia for the Colorado goldfields in 1860 and they never saw him again. He found no gold either in Colorado or Montana Territory, but in 1864 he and partner John Jacob blazed a trail connecting the Oregon Trail with Bannack in the heart of the Montana goldfields. The Bozeman Trail, while a shorter route, cut through the prime hunting grounds of the Crow, Sioux, and Northern Cheyenne, and they didn't like it. The trail proved so dangerous it became known as the Bloody Bozeman, and by 1867 the US Army gave up trying to protect its travelers and all but the foolhardy quit using it.

The trail began in the vicinity of present Casper, Wyoming, and wound through a mountain pass into the fertile Gallatin Valley before continuing to the gold country. Bozeman began farming in the valley and became one of the founders of the town that soon bore his name. Only he wouldn't be around to relish the honor. In April 1867 Bozeman and another man were killed by Indians along the Yellowstone River near present Livingston.

Protected by nearby Fort Ellis, Bozeman developed as a commercial hub for area farms and mining operations. When the Northern Pacific Railroad began serving the city in 1883, it became a gateway to Yellowstone National Park, and in 1893 the state legislature made it the home of Montana State University.

The remains of John Bozeman (1835–1867) were returned to Bozeman and buried in **Sunset Hills Cemetery**. From East Main Street, turn south on Buttonwood Avenue; the cemetery is at the end of the street directly south of Lindley Park.

Henry T.P. Comstock

A way-down-on-his-luck former prospector named Henry T.P. Comstock committed suicide in Bozeman on September 27, 1870.

Or did he?

While most accounts have his death as self-inflicted, since his body was found outside a saloon, a minority opinion holds that he had been robbed and killed. No one claimed his body, so he was buried in Sunset Hills Cemetery, adjacent to the Nelson Story family plots. It's the inscription on his grave marker that tells the rest of the story: "Here Lies Henry T.P. Comstock, founder of the Comstock Lode, Storey County, Nevada." Comstock made $11,000 after selling his Nevada silver claim and lost that in a business deal. The mine and others produced millions of dollars of silver.

Built at a cost of $100,000 and opened in 1891, the **Bozeman Hotel** (321 East Main St.) had 136 rooms equipped with the latest in urban comforts—even an elevator. When the hotel opened, the *Bozeman Chronicle* declared it "the most elaborate, complete and comfortable caravansary so far constructed in the state." Investors and civic boosters hoped voters would be selecting Bozeman as the state capital, but Helena held on as the seat of government. The hotel continued as a "caravansary" until the 1970s. New owners remodeled the building, and it is now used for office space.

First known as the McGill Museum for its founder, Butte, Montana, physician Dr. Caroline McGill, the **Museum of the Rockies** (600 West Kagy Blvd.; 406-994-2682) opened in 1957. Jointly operated by Montana State University and a nonprofit group, the museum is a Smithsonian affiliate. It focuses on paleontology, Rocky Mountain wildlife, regional history, and the history of Yellowstone National Park.

BUTTE (SILVER BOW COUNTY)

The rich history of Butte is an alchemy of happenstance that turned a little gold into a middling amount of silver into a bonanza of copper. Placer mining began along Silver Bow Creek in 1864, but the gold play never amounted to much. But in the mid-1870s the mining camp that became Butte did experience a short-lived silver boom. Then, in 1881, silver mine owner Marcus Daly found copper sulfide at the three-hundred-foot level. It proved to be the largest copper deposit ever found, and Butte boomed like it never had. By the turn of the twentieth century, it had a multi-national population of forty-seven thousand and surpassed Leadville, Colorado, as the West's most active mining town.

The Butte mines ran around the clock and so did the city's numerous saloons and brothels. Ruthless conflict between cooper mine owners, labor issues, and ethnic clashes added to the violence always attendant to wide-open bars and prostitution. The Rev. William Biederwolf called Butte "the lowest sinkhole of vice in the west [with] enough legitimate vice . . . to damn the souls of every young man and young woman in it." But brothel owners kept police and city officials paid off, and the madams and sex workers helped support Butte's more traditional businesses, so the city took its time in ending widespread vice. Butte remains a copper mining town.

With more than six thousand historic buildings, Butte is the largest National Historic Landmark District in the nation. The **Butte**

Convention and Visitor Bureau (1000 George St.; 406-723-3177) has maps and brochures on the city's historic sites and other attractions. The **World Museum of Mining** (155 Museum Way; 406-723-7211) is on twenty-two acres around an inactive silver and zinc mine, the Orphan Girl. Founded as a nonprofit organization in 1964, the museum opened in 1965.

All western mining and railroad towns had an Asian population, mostly Chinese. Butte had a large Chinese community, though only a few families remained by the mid-twentieth century. Operated by the Mai Wai Society, a nonprofit dedicated to preserving the Rocky Mountain West's Asian history, the **Mai Wai Society Museum** (17 West Mercury St.; 406-723-3231) fills two historic brick buildings once part of Butte's Chinatown. One was a mercantile store dating to the 1890s and the other, in a 1905 building, was a noodle parlor. With more than 2,500 items once stocked in the old store, in addition to other objects and photographs related to Butte's Asian history, the museum also displays 140 artifacts representative of the 60,000 recovered during a 2007 archaeological dig in the heart of what used to be Butte's Chinatown.

One of Montana's big-three copper kings was W.A. Clark, who, beginning in 1884 and continuing until 1888, built a thirty-four-room Romanesque Revival–style residence known today either as the W.A. Clark Mansion or the **Copper King Mansion** (219 West Granite St.; 406-782-7580). The mansion is listed on the National Register of Historic Places. The privately owned residence is a bed-and-breakfast, but tours are given.

Butte's most storied—and long-lived—brothel was opened in 1890 by French Canadian brothers Joseph and Arthur Nadeau and named for Joseph's wife, Delia Dumas Nadeau. With a succession of owners, the brothel continued to operate, albeit much more discreetly, as most of the city's red-light district was shut down. Clearly a Butte institution, the brothel stayed in business until 1982. The two-story brick building is operated as the **Dumas Brothel Museum** (45 East Mercury St.; 406-351-9922).

CASCADE (CASCADE COUNTY)

The first post office here was designated as Dodge, but when the Montana Central Railroad came through in 1886, the name of the community was changed to Cascade. Fifteen miles west of the future town, in 1862 the Jesuits established St. Peter's Mission to minister to the Blackfeet people. The mission evolved into a school for American Indian girls in the late 1870s. In 1884, Ursuline nuns came from Toledo, Ohio, to teach at St. Peter's. Not everyone at the mission wore a habit.

Mary Fields Drove a Stagecoach

Born a slave in the early 1830s somewhere in the South—exactly when and where has never been determined—Mary Fields spent the rest of her days following emancipation relishing the freedom to live life her way.

Working as a cook on steamboats after the Civil War, the six-foot tall, heavy-set woman traveled the Mississippi before settling in Toledo, Ohio. There she found work in the Ursuline Convent of the Sacred Heart, becoming friends with Mother Superior Amadeus Dunne. When Mother Amadeus left Ohio for St. Peter's Mission, Mary went to Montana with her.

At the new convent Mary did everything from laundry to maintenance to gardening. She also procured and delivered supplies, hauling goods to the convent by wagon. A good shot, she kept the convent supplied with fresh game. But it was hard for the sisters to ignore Mary's licentious lifestyle. At nearby Cascade, she frequented saloons—smoking and drinking heavily—and otherwise lived a decidedly unholy life. After quick-tempered Mary pulled a gun on a male janitor during an argument at the convent, her patron fired her.

In Cascade on her own, Mary variously ran an eatery, took in laundry, and did odd jobs to support herself. But in 1895 she got a post office contract as a rural mail carrier, making her deliveries in a stagecoach drawn by five horses and a mule she named Moses. And that's how she came to be known as **Stagecoach**

Mary, the first black mail carrier in US history. For eight years, she made the thirty-four-mile round-trip between Cascade and the mission, never missing a day. When heavy snow precluded the use of her stagecoach, she delivered mail wearing snowshoes.

Despite her rough character, Mary was well regarded in and around Cascade. When she died of liver disease in 1914, townspeople collected money to pay for her funeral. She is buried in Cascade's **Hillside Cemetery.** A large rock inscribed only "Mary Fields/1832-1914" marks her grave.

CHINOOK (BLAINE COUNTY)

Sixteen miles south of Chinook on County Road 240, the site of the **Battle of Bear Paw** is part of the four-state **Nez Perce National Historic Park.**

The desperate 126-day flight of the Nez Perce under Chief Joseph ended only forty miles below their destination of Canada at a point the Indians called "Place of the Manure Fire." Later it became known as Bear Paw Battlefield. Cornered by soldiers under Col. Nelson A. Miles, the Nez Perce lost their horses the first day of the engagement, September 30, 1877. Still, they resisted two bloody attacks and held off the troops until October 5, when Chief Joseph surrendered.

The **Blaine County Historical Museum** (501 Indiana St.; 406-375-2590) has an exhibit on the battle as well as displays on other aspects of the area's history.

DEER LODGE (POWELL COUNTY)

Laid out in 1862 as LaBarge City, two years later the town's name changed to Deer Lodge, after the surrounding Deer Lodge Valley. Five years after the organization of Montana Territory in 1864, the Montana Territorial Prison opened here in 1869. Primarily a ranching trade center and a prison town, Deer Lodge got an economic boost in 1910 after gaining a railroad connection.

The Montana territorial legislature appropriated money for a prison at Deer Lodge in 1869 with prisoners doing the labor. The facility opened in 1871, and was expanded in 1877 and shored up with a new wall in 1893, but the place was always underfunded and run by political hacks with no experience. Consequently, the prison was a hellhole. It later got professional management, but it was poorly built, never had enough operating money, and generally did not distinguish itself among the nation's other penal institutions. Despite all its problems, the prison remained in use for 108 years until the state built a new facility a few miles outside of town.

The old prison (1106 Main St.; 406-846-3111) houses four museums related to the Old West: **Old Montana Prison Museum, Powell County Museum, Frontier Montana Museum,** and **Yesterday's Playthings Museum.**

The Grant-Kohrs Ranch

Montana was and is big ranch country. John Grant, whose father had been an early fur trader, in 1859 built a cabin in the western end of the fifty-five-mile-long, mountain-bound meadow known as Deer Lodge Valley. Buying worn-out cattle from westbound travelers along the Oregon Trail, Grant built up a herd and began selling beef to the mining camps in the area. Three years later, doing well, he moved his ranch to the east end of the valley near where the town of Deer Lodge would later develop.

Grant built a nice two-story ranch house in 1862, but in 1866 he sold his ranch to Denmark immigrant Conrad Kohrs. Kohrs expanded the ranch house and the ranch, turning it into a cattle-raising empire. He sold the ranch in 1918, and it was inactive until Kohrs's grandson, Conrad Kohrs Warren, gained control of the ranch in 1940 and became a noted producer of Hereford and shorthorn cattle. Warren conveyed the ranch to the National Park Service in 1972.

On the northwest edge of Deer Lodge, the 1,618-acre **Grant-Kohrs Ranch National Historic Site** (251 Grant Circle;

406-846-2070) is still maintained as a working cattle ranch. In addition to a visitor center with interpretive exhibits and artifacts, the site includes eighty-eight historic structures, from the Victorian-style ranch house to a cowboy's bunkhouse.

DILLON (BEAVERHEAD COUNTY)

Rancher Richard Deacon did something not a lot of men did: He said "no" to a railroad company. When the Utah and Northern Railroad (later part of the Union Pacific) approached him in 1880 to purchase a right-of-way through his property, he told the company it could buy his entire 480-acre ranch or find another route. Not about to accept that deal, the railroad would take a different route. But a group of businessmen were willing to buy Deacon's ranch. Then they donated the right-of-way to the railroad and had the ranchland surveyed as a townsite. Deacon got $10,500 for his property. When the new owners auctioned lots that October, they made their money back plus $4,000 in profit.

Named for Union Pacific president Sidney Dillon, the town prospered as a shipping point and commercial center, and in 1881 took the county seat away from the already legendary gold mining town of Bannack. The **Beaverhead County Museum** (15 South Montana St.; 406-683-5027) focuses on local history.

Battle of the Big Hole

The history of the Old West has no shortage of tragic events, but one of the most tragic episodes of the Indian Wars took place here on August 9–10, 1877, when US soldiers executed a surprise attack on some 750 Nez Perce in what came to be called the Battle of the Big Hole. An estimated seventy to ninety men, women, and children died in the engagement.

Sixty-five miles northwest of Dillon, and ten miles west of Wisdom, **Big Hole National Battlefield** (16425 State Highway 43

West, Wisdom; 406-689-3155) has a visitor center with artifacts and interpretive exhibits overlooking the battlefield. Self-guided trails lead to key points marked with interpretive signs.

Montana Governor R.B. Smith and other state officials attended the grand opening of **Hotel Metlen** (5 South Railroad Ave.; 406-683-2335) on February 11, 1898, an event the local newspaper hailed as "the beginning of a new epoch in the history of Dillon." The *Dillon Tribune* went on to note that the three-story brick hotel built by "the genial" J.C. Metlen "is beautifully furnished throughout and possesses all the modern conveniences, such as steam heat, hot and cold water and electric lights." The hotel also had a private parlor for ladies. Built to accommodate rail travelers, the hotel faces the Union Pacific tracks. It is listed on the National Register of Historic Places.

ELKHORN (JEFFERSON COUNTY)

In 1870, Swiss-born prospector Peter Wys discovered rich silver ore near future Elkhorn. Wys died before he could capitalize on his find, but Helena capitalist Anton Holter did. His Elkhorn Mine produced millions of dollars in silver before he sold it in 1888 to British investors. The mine was earning $30,000 a month when the value of silver crashed in 1893. Within sixty days, three of every four of the town's 2,500 residents had left town. The post office closed in 1924, though some minor mining continued in the area until the early 1950s.

In 1967 an article in *Old West Magazine* said, "If you could visit only one ghost town in the West, this old Montana settlement would come close to epitomizing all the false-front excitement of yesterday." But no longer. As Philip Varney put it in his 2010 book, *Ghost Towns of the Mountain West*, "time, weather, fire, and capitalism" have taken a significant toll on the historical integrity of the town since the early 1970s. Still, two of its early false-front buildings are impressive: the 1880s-vintage Gillian Hall, which had retail businesses on the first floor with a saloon and dance hall on the second floor; and Fraternity

Hall, the town's 1893 community center. The two buildings comprise Montana's smallest state park, opened in 1980.

Elkhorn State Park (812 Elkhorn St.; 406-495-3270; GPS coordinates: N46° 16.51', W111° 56.77') can be reached from Boulder, south of Helena. Take State Highway 69 south for seven miles, turn left, and cross a small bridge before turning right on a gravel road. Follow the road, bearing left at each of two forks in the road, for thirteen miles to Elkhorn.

FORT BENTON (CHOUTEAU COUNTY)

Called the "Chicago of the Plains" for several heady decades, Fort Benton could boast of being the world's innermost port. Steamboats plying the Missouri River made it the bustling supply hub of the Northern Plains, its merchants enjoying a vast trade territory stretching from Canada to Washington Territory. The town began in 1850 as a fur trading post on the south side of the Missouri named for US senator Thomas Hart Benton, though fur trader Alexander Culbertson had been operating in the general area (but on the north side of the river) since 1845. Business picked up even more when placer mining began in western Montana in the 1860s, and the town continued to flourish until the arrival of the Northern Pacific Railroad in the early 1880s. Like all riverboat towns, Fort Benton in its heyday was rougher than a rocky bottom in shallow water. One local newspaper called it "a scalp market, home of cutthroats and horse thieves."

The **Museum of the Northern Great Plains** (1205 20th St.; http://fortbentonmuseums.com/the-museums/museum-of-the-northern-great-plains/) displays six mounted buffalo preserved for the Smithsonian Institution in Washington in 1886. Taken by William T. Hornaday in 1879, from the last wild herd in Montana outside Yellowstone National Park, they were returned to Montana in 1955, then restored and put back on exhibit in 1996. **Homestead Village**, a collection of restored historic structures, and the **Montana Agriculture Center** also are part of the museum. **Old Fort Benton** (1900 River St.), in Old Fort Park, is a reconstruction of the 1850 trading post and its chief trader's house. The **Museum of the Upper Missouri River** is also part of Old Fort Park. The **Missouri Breaks National Monument Interpretive Center** (701 7th St.; 406-622-5316) has the rifle that Chief Joseph surrendered to Gen. Nelson Miles on October 7, 1877, at the Bear Paw Battlefield.

Too Helpful for His Own Good

Bill Hynson belonged to the vigilantes, who had already rid Fort Benton of two undesirables. But while holding himself forth as a law-and-order proponent, he supplemented his income by removing money from the pockets of passed-out drunks. Some of Hynson's fellow self-designated crime fighters suspected him of as much, so they got someone to pretend to be in a drunken stupor to see what Hynson would do. What he did was rob the man. When their undercover operative reported what happened, the vigilantes determined that the riverboat town needed yet another hanging. While sworn to enforce the law, the town marshal and his deputy also belonged to the mob. When someone alerted the deputy that another bad apple would soon be removed from the barrel, not knowing the honoree's identity, the lawman happened to mention the pending necktie party to Hynson. The thief righteously offered to furnish the rope. Not only that, he would have a grave dug for the scoundrel. To Hynson's great surprise, when he handed the rope over to the marshal, the officer promptly put the noose around his neck and the mob dragged him off to the nearest tree. Soon strangled with his own rope, Hynson then filled the grave he had so graciously readied for some crook.

Hynson and the other vigilante victims likely ended up in **Riverside Cemetery,** one of Montana's oldest burial grounds. The cemetery is still there, but there are no grave markers and burial records have been lost.

Built at a cost of $50,000, plus an additional $150,000 for its furnishings, the three-story stone **Grand Union Hotel** (1 Grand Union Sq.; 406-622-1882) was indeed grand. Opened in 1882 with the biggest celebration Montana had seen to that point in its history, the hostelry stands as a monument to false optimism. When the Great Northern Railway approached Fort Benton, the business community assumed the town would continue as a transportation center. Hoping also to become the territory's capital, civic leaders believed an accommodation like the Grand would lay figurative tracks toward new growth. But riverboats could not compete with trains and the town dried up as a port. Nor did Fort Benton get the capital. The hotel continued in business until closing in the mid-1980s. New owners restored it to its former elegance in the late 1990s and reopened it in 1999.

GARNET (GRANITE COUNTY)

Considered the second-best-preserved ghost town in Montana, with more than thirty old buildings, Garnet looks like a Western movie set. But the former mining town is not as old as it looks, even if visually impressive. Placer gold had been discovered in the Garnet Range of west-central Montana in the 1870s, but no significant mining took place in the area until the mid- to late 1890s. A community grew around a stamp mill opened by Armistead Mitchell in 1895 and took his name. When a post office opened there two years later, the town's name was changed to Garnet for the ruby-like mineral found in the area. The real boom came in 1898 with the opening of the lucrative Nancy Hanks Mine. Unlike most western mining towns, Garnet— thanks mostly to a strong union presence—developed as a law-abiding community, its jail mostly accommodating the occasional drunk. By 1905 Garnet's boom had gone bust, and a destructive fire in 1912 drove off more residents. Mining picked up again during the Great Depression, but that ended with World War II. The post office closed in 1942, and the last resident died five years later. Efforts to preserve the old town began in 1970. The 134-acre Garnet Historic District was listed on the National Register of Historic Places in 2010.

Twenty miles east of Missoula, Garnet can be reached from State Highway 200. Turn south at the "Garnet Ghost Town" sign between mile markers 22 and 23 and follow the gravel road eleven miles to Garnet. This is not an all-weather road, so check local conditions first. The ghost town is managed by the federal Bureau of Land Management and the nonprofit Garnet Preservation Association. A visitor center (406-329-3914) has a self-guided walking tour.

GREAT FALLS (CASCADE COUNTY)

Though the great falls of the Missouri River had been known since the days of Lewis and Clark, the city of Great Falls was not founded until 1883. Envisioning a hydropower-driven industrial city, flour merchant Paris Gibson had a townsite platted and the community grew steadily. A scenic setting, despite a smelter and other industries, Great Falls attracted its most famous resident—Charles Marion Russell.

Charlie Russell, as the old expression goes, knew which end of a cow gets up first. Russell (1864–1926) was born in St. Louis but as a teenager went to Montana in 1880 to become a cowboy. And that's what he did, spending more than a decade as a wrangler before turning to something else he got to be good at: art.

Over the course of his career, Russell produced more than four thousand works portraying the Old West—oil paintings, watercolors, sculptures, and artistry of another sort, written words. Russell died at his home in Grand Falls in the fall of 1926.

Founded in 1953 and much expanded over the years, the **C.M. Russell Museum** (400 13th St. North; 406-727-8787) curates one of the largest collections of Russell's work. Covering a square block, the museum complex includes the artist's restored 1903 log studio and the home he and his wife Nancy Cooper Russell built in Great Falls in 1900. In addition to roughly a thousand works of art produced by Russell, the museum has a large collection of Western art in general. Beyond exhibits devoted to Russell's work and life, the museum has a permanent exhibit on the buffalo, firearms, and other aspects of the West Russell knew and loved.

Operated by the Cascade County Historical Society, the **High Plains Heritage Center** (422 2nd St.; 406-452-3462) has interpretive exhibits on all aspects of High Plains history and culture. Its holdings include more than ninety-five thousand artifacts and a large repository of archival material.

The Lewis and Clark Expedition spent just over a month in the area, longer than at any other of their non-winter camps. The **Lewis and Clark National Historic Trail Interpretive Center** (4201 Giant Springs Rd.; 406-727-8733) was opened in 1998 and expanded in 2003. With 5,500 square feet, the center is considered one of the most comprehensive Lewis and Clark museums.

HELENA (LEWIS AND CLARK COUNTY)

Only one city in the world has a street, let alone a main street, called Last Chance Gulch—the capital of Montana. And few cities could have a more appropriately named thoroughfare.

Four down-on-their-luck gold prospectors who had repeatedly struck out at striking it rich made camp July 14, 1864, on a small stream in northwestern Montana Territory known as Prickly Pear Creek. Not long after, Reginald Stanley walked upstream with pick and shovel to give it one last shot. This time the men were in luck. Digging down to bedrock, Stanley found a handful of gold nuggets, and within weeks the rush was on. Last Chance Gulch—as they came to call it—along with other gulches in the general area, produced more than $15 million in gold before the placer mining played out. Hard-rock mining in the area kept the bonanza going even longer.

Last Chance Gulch became the new town's main drag, but miners thought the community needed a more traditional name, so they decided on Helena after a town in Minnesota where one of them came from. Though plagued by a series of devastating fires, Helena grew and in 1875 became the territorial capital. Nineteen years later it won an election to become Montana's permanent seat of government.

The **Helena Visitor Center** (105 Reeder's Alley; 406-449-2107) has a self-guided tour of the city's historic downtown along with maps and brochures on historic sites and other attractions.

Hanging Tree

Many a tree across the Wild West served to suspend necktie party honorees, but over the years Helena's hanging tree saw the extra-judicial hanging of seven to eleven, depending on the telling.

On April 30, 1872—as distant thunder warned of an approaching rainstorm—the tree accommodated two men at one time, Arthur L. Compton and Joseph Wilson. The duo had robbed and shot rancher George Lenhart three days before. Unfortunately for them, Lenhart had lived long enough to say who shot him. The sheriff duly placed the pair in jail, but public sentiment favored more speedy adjudication. A group of men assembled, removed the two men from jail, tried them, and then strung them up. The tree stood for years but was finally cut down by a preacher who was concerned that due to its age it might fall on his church. There is no historical marker.

Fires posed such a proven risk to Helena that in 1874 the city built a wooden fire tower on high ground overlooking the town. The structure didn't prevent fires from breaking out, but it enabled the alarm to spread faster. Now known as the **Guardian of the Gulch,** the old tower still stands just south of Broadway on Cruse Avenue.

A respectable number of late nineteenth-century Helena residents were quite well off and lived in expensive, impressive homes on the city's west side. Many of their old Victorian mansions still stand in an area bounded by Benton, Lawrence, Monroe, and Stuart Streets, now known as the Mansion District.

Across the street from the copper-domed 1902 **Montana Capitol** (1301 East 6th Ave.), the **Montana Historical Society Museum** (225 North Roberts St.; 406-444-2694) covers twelve thousand years of human history. The historical society also maintains the original governor's mansion, a two-story 1888 Queen Anne–style house at 304 North Ewing Street. It was used by nine of the state's chief executives from 1913 to 1959.

Lewistown (Fergus County)

Settlement in this area of central Montana began with a trading post established in 1873, but the town was not platted until the early 1880s.

Its tents and wood-frame buildings long gone, Lewistown's downtown historic district is listed on the National Register of Historical Places. The **Central Montana Historical Museum** (408 NE Main St.; 406-535-3642) is operated by the nonprofit Central Montana Historical Association.

Best Not to Mess with Uncle Sam

When the two horse thieves rode into one-year-old Lewistown, they passed new false-front wooden businesses draped in red, white, and blue bunting in observance of Independence Day, 1884. Not particularly patriotic, Charles "Rattlesnake Jake" Fallon and Charles "Longhair" Owens were more interested in celebrating what they saw as their inalienable right to get drunk. Spotting a young man dressed as Uncle Sam, they roughed him up and made him crawl in the dirt down the town's busy main street. Throwing in some fireworks, the pair fired their guns in the general direction of the crowd that had gathered. Not hitting anyone, they went inside one of the town's several saloons to have a drink or two.

Meanwhile, a delegation of annoyed citizens went to a hardware store where the proprietor readily supplied them with rifles and ammunition. When the two drunk bullies swaggered out of the bar, gunfire erupted. Bullets flying, the pair hoofed it in the direction of a photographer's tent. There they made their last stand. Though seriously outgunned, "Rattlesnake" and "Longhair" kept shooting until they died.

When the bodies were laid out so the photographer could take their picture, onlookers counted nine bullet holes in Fallon and five in Owens. As soon as the photography session ended, the pair was unceremoniously buried on the edge of town. No one bothered to put up a grave marker, but the bodies were later exhumed and taken farther out of town for reburial. Someone kept at least one of the outlaws' skulls as a souvenir. In 1969 the skull was donated to the Central Montana Museum where it remains on display.

LIVINGSTON (PARK COUNTY)

Other than a brief stay by Captain William Clark of the Lewis and Clark Expedition in 1806, the first Euro-American settlement in the area that would become Livingston was Benson's Landing, a trading post on the Yellowstone River. Livingston developed later with the arrival of the Northern Pacific in the summer of 1882. The town started out as Clark City for Herman Clark, a railroad contractor. That fall, Clark City moved from where the old trading post had been to a point three miles upstream and was renamed Livingston for Northern Pacific stockholder and director Johnston Livingston. Soon Livingston served as a division point for the railroad with shops to service its steam engines and cars.

The new town prospered even more when the railroad ran a line south to Yellowstone National Park. That made the town, as the business community happily proclaimed, "The Gateway to Yellowstone."

Two museums focused on railroading, Livingston history in general, and the town's connection to Yellowstone National Park are the **Livingston Depot Center** (200 West Park St.; 406-222-2300) and the **Yellowstone Gateway Museum of Park County** (118 West Chinook St.; 406-222-4184).

"Can't You Tell a Lady Where She Lives?"

Calamity Jane lived for a time in Livingston and frequently made the pages of the local newspaper. Nearly two decades after she died in 1903, a former Livingston reporter recalled an encounter he had with the well-known Western character.

Walking back to his room in the Albemarle Hotel late one night, Lewis R. Freeman noticed a cowboy "in the act of embracing a lamp post." He intended to walk on by until a rough voice said, "Short Pants! Can't you tell a lady where she lives?" Freeman moved closer to the circle of light around the post. "Show me where the lady is and I'll try," he replied. "She's me, Short Pants—Martha Canary—Martha Burk, better known as Calamity Jane."

Freeman soon understood the woman's situation: She was too drunk to remember where she was staying, other than it was a second-floor room above one of the town's numerous saloons. Freeman chivalrously took her from bar to bar, gathering volunteers along the way, until they finally found Calamity's room. Since she had also lost her key, they had to boost her through a window to get her inside. The following day, in appreciation, Calamity granted the young reporter an interview. But first, she said, he'd need to buy her a bucket of beer.

The journalist interviewed her over a period of several days. One morning when he went to meet her for another session, he learned she had donned her buckskins, picked up her horse at the livery stable, and ridden off toward Big Timber. Not only had she earlier forgotten where she was staying, she "forgot" to pay her rent before leaving town, Freeman recalled. "I never heard of her again until the papers, a year or two later, had word of her death." His recollection of the time he spent with Calamity appeared in the *Livingston Enterprise*, June 24, 1922.

When she wasn't rooming above a saloon, Calamity Jane lived in a log cabin at 222 South Main. For years the cabin bore a sign reading, "Once The Home of Calamity Jane The Oldest Building In Livingston." Badly deteriorated, the cabin was torn down in 1934.

LOLO (MISSOULA COUNTY)

On June 9, 1805, members of the Lewis and Clark Expedition made camp near where Lolo Creek flows into the Bitterroot River. Not far from a hot spring long favored by American Indians, Meriwether Lewis wrote in his journal that they had decided to call their campsite

"Travellers Rest." The corps spent two nights here, resting their horses (as well as themselves) and taking "celestial observations." They camped here again in late June and early July the following year on their way back east.

The general area of Travelers' Rest had been designated as a National Historic Landmark in 1960 and added to the National Register of Historic Places six years later. However, not until the early twenty-first century were archaeologists finally able to pinpoint where Lewis and Clark had camped. A 2002 archaeological dig at the site found traces of mercury, a non-deteriorating element that does not occur naturally in the area. Further investigation revealed that the mercury came from the excretion of two expedition members who had taken a laxative called Dr. Rush's Pills. The pills, 1,300 doses having been generously provided for the expedition by Dr. Benjamin Rush, did their job so well that they came to be called "Rush's Thunderbolts." Records of the expedition show that Lewis often administered the medicine.

Based on the findings, the boundaries of **Travelers' Rest State Park** (6717 US 12 West; 406-273-4253) were expanded to include the actual campsite. (Archaeologists also found the expedition's campfire remnants and a few artifacts, making it only the second Lewis and Clark camping site documented by scientific evidence.)

After leaving Travelers' Rest, the expedition continued west toward the Pacific, crossing the Continental Divide through what is now known as Lolo Pass. The **Lolo Pass Visitor Center** (twenty-eight miles west of Lolo on US 12 at the Montana-Idaho border) has interpretive exhibits on the Lewis and Clark Expedition and the Nez Perce.

The **Holt Heritage Museum** (6800 US 12; 406-273-6743), as its website summarizes, is devoted to "Cowboys & Indians – Rodeos and Pow Wows." The museum was founded by Bill and Ramona Holt—Bill a longtime rodeo announcer, Ramona a longtime rodeo performer.

MALTA (PHILLIPS COUNTY)

Only forty-five miles below the Canadian border, Malta was the Wild West's northernmost cow town. Surrounded by grassland in the Milk River valley, Malta was favored by local ranchers and Texas cattlemen as a place to fatten their herds in summer. Cowboys being cowboys, Malta became their whoop-it-up town. The area's first settler was Robert M. Trafton, who in 1887 moved his trading post to the town's present location to be on the Great Northern Railway tracks. The town didn't get a name until the railroad came. The story goes that the railroad came up with a name by blindfolding an employee at its St. Paul, Minnesota, headquarters and asking him to point his finger at some part of the globe. That spot proved to be Malta, an island in the Mediterranean.

The Wild Bunch's Last Robbery

The Wild Bunch went out with a bang.

Several of them.

On July 3, 1901, a gunman got on the westbound Great Northern Railway's Coast Flyer when the express passenger train stopped at the depot in Wagner. When the train left the station, he crawled over the tender, commandeered the locomotive, and ordered the engineer to stop the train. Other bandits who had been waiting at the predetermined robbery site forced the train crew to separate the express car from the rest of the train.

All this was according to plan, but then the shooting started.

When two trainmen ran down the tracks to ignite flares to prevent another train from crashing into the stopped passenger train, gang members opened fire. Both railroad men were hit, one of them later dying. During the shooting, a stray bullet also hit a young woman passenger in her shoulder.

Returning their attention to the express car, the robbers used dynamite to blow open the safe and collected around $40,000 before galloping away. Though for years Butch Cassidy and the Sundance Kid got credit for the robbery, most historians believe both outlaws were in South America by then. Harvey Logan, aka Kid Curry, was the bandit who orchestrated the robbery.

The robbery occurred about ten miles west of Malta, near Wagner. Nothing marks the site and Wagner is all but a ghost town. But the **Phillips County Museum** (432 US 2 East; 406-654-1037) has an exhibit on Kid Curry and other Wild Bunch members, including pistols, wanted posters, newspaper clippings, and photographs.

MILES CITY (CUSTER COUNTY)

Gen. Nelson A. Miles had a war to win. Most of Lt. Col. George Armstrong Custer's command had been annihilated at the Little Bighorn that summer of 1876, and Miles knew hard campaigns lay ahead. But late that year, in addition to the hostile Sioux and other Plains Indians, the general faced another foe: whiskey and its impact on his soldiers. Accordingly, Miles ordered all the booze-selling civilians, gamblers, loafers, and other unsavory types to leave the garrison he commanded, Tongue River Cantonment. Miles placed a marker two miles from the post and told the riffraff to set up their tents there. Evidently not insulted by the bum's rush, the refugees named their new camp Miles City in honor of the man who had thrown them out.

The following year, Miles moved his troops to a better location two miles west of where the Tongue River met the Yellowstone River. The new post would be called Fort Keogh in honor of Capt. Myles Keogh, one of the cavalry officers who had fallen with Custer. When the troops moved, Miles City followed to its present location.

The army had the Indian situation under control by 1878, but Fort Keogh remained an active post until 1910, when it became a remount station for the acquisition and training of cavalry horses. After World War I, the military permanently abandoned the post.

Little Bighorn Battlefield National Monument

During the long clash of cultures collectively known as the Indian Wars, the US Army had numerous engagements with hostile tribes, but none are better remembered than the battle with Lakota Sioux under Sitting Bull in which half the Seventh Cavalry died or were wounded.

Each of the 267 soldiers had a different story, but on June 25, 1876, their personal narratives reached a common final chapter on the grassy plains of southeastern Montana Territory.

Twenty-one-year-old James Henry Russell, born in Corpus Christi, Texas, in January 1852 and raised in Florida, was teaching school in Boston when he decided to join the army. Nothing in what little is known of him reveals why the five-foot-five bachelor made such a drastic career change, but it may have been because his father had served in the military during the Seminole Indian War and later fought for the Confederacy. On the other hand, perhaps the young educator, having tired of the classroom, longed for adventure in the still very wild West. Whatever his motivation, on September 11, 1873, Russell enlisted in the Seventh Cavalry. After riding with the army's best-known regiment under one of its best-known officers for nearly three years, Private Russell died with Lt. Col. George Armstrong Custer and most of the rest of his command on June 25, 1876, in the Battle of the Little Bighorn. Russell fell on what came to be known as Last Stand Hill, one of forty or so soldiers—including Custer—who fought hard to the very last.

First buried where he fell, in 1878 Russell's remains and those of his comrades were removed and placed in a mass grave at the top of the hill. In 1881, a large gray granite monument engraved with the names of all those killed in the fight was placed at the center of the hill above the reinterred remains. Russell is listed on the stone's east face, the sixteenth name down from the top in the left column. The battlefield was designated as Custer National Cemetery, and over the years, as military garrisons in the region were abandoned, the remains of other soldiers were reinterred there. As the number of visitors to the cemetery increased, in 1940 the War Department transferred the property to the National Park Service. The NPS began managing it as a national monument in 1946.

The known facts of the battle have not changed much since then (though twenty-first-century archaeological work at the site added some definition to the picture), but how those facts are interpreted has changed. In 2003, a striking stone and steel memorial to the American Indians who took part in the battle was dedicated, a lasting reminder that brave men on both sides died in that distant day's bloody fighting. Twelve years before, in a first official reflection of the more balanced way of looking at the engagement, the name of the site was changed from Custer Battlefield National Monument to **Little Bighorn Battlefield National Monument.**

The battle site is sixty-two miles east of Billings (135 miles southwest of Miles City) at Crow Agency on the Crow Indian Reservation. Take I-90 East to US 212 and turn north to the monument entrance. Exhibits, artifacts, and a video in the visitor center (406-638-3216) tell the story of the battle. Self-guided walking and driving tours are available there.

The Sioux may have been subjugated, but not Miles City. By 1880 the town had twenty-three saloons and one church that was about to be built. In addition to the soldiers from the nearby fort, Miles City also catered to cowboys, sheepherders, buffalo hunters, and railroaders. As an early Montana highway marker said of the town, "She was wild for a while. [In] . . . the 1880s . . . many a Texas trail herd came through here and the city soon acquired a national reputation as a cattle and horse market which it has never relinquished."

Founded in 1939, the **Range Rider Museum** (435 I-94 Business; 406-232-6146) is a private collection covering the whole range of eastern Montana history, from the area's early American Indian inhabitants, through the Fort Keogh era, the development of cattle and sheep ranching, and the coming of the railroad. In addition to its other artifacts, the museum is home to the Bert Clark gun collection of more than four hundred firearms. For more than twenty-five years, Bob and Betty Ann Barthelmess operated the museum. Their daughter Bunny Miller continues the tradition.

MISSOULA (MISSOULA COUNTY)

French fur trappers called the narrow valley *Porte de l'Enfer,* "Gate of Hell." That's because the Blackfeet Indians often ambushed travelers there, as evidenced by human bones trappers saw scattered over the area. In 1860, when Christopher Higgins and Francis Worden established a trading post near the canyon, they named it Hell Gate. The small settlement that developed there lived up to its name. During the village's four-year life, nine lynchings occurred there. As one visiting nineteenth-century journalist wrote of Hell Gate, "Its people were strong and healthy. Those who died, died quickly and without the preliminary of being sick." In 1864, Higgins and Worden moved their operation four miles to the site of present Missoula. The town, protected from Indians by Fort Missoula after its establishment in 1877, developed as an agricultural trade center until the legislature located the University of Montana there in 1893, stimulating further growth.

During the fading years of the Wild West, the storied Buffalo Soldiers of the Twenty-fifth Infantry Division in 1896 took on a little-known mission—they became the US Army Bicycle Corps. With a bicycle craze sweeping the nation, it occurred to someone in the army that a bicycle did not have to be watered, fed, or stabled. Accordingly, hand-picked soldiers underwent training at Fort Missoula in bike riding that included getting themselves and their bike over a nine-foot fence. Next, the unit took a 126-mile round-trip from the fort to Lake McDonald, in present Glacier National Park. Lt. James Moss then took the corps to Yellowstone National Park, completing a 790-mile trip in a little over two weeks. After riding from Fort Missoula to St. Louis in thirty-four days, Lieutenant Moss declared the unit ready for modern warfare. But before that could happen, the development of motorcycles relegated pedal-powered machines to civilian use.

Thirteen historic buildings still stand at the former post, where the **Historical Museum at Fort Missoula** (3400 Captain Rawn Way; 406-728-3476) interprets the post's history. Also located there is the **Rocky Mountain Museum of Military History** (Buildings T-310 and T-316, Fort Missoula; 406-549-5346).

Mother Gleim

As a madam, Mary Gleim made her living selling feminine companionship, but she was not the most ladylike of bordello owners and, at three hundred pounds, certainly not petite. She did time in 1894 for trying to kill a woman who happened to be interested in her man at the time, and she supplemented her "female boardinghouse" earnings by smuggling everything from diamonds to Chinese workers. She kept her two establishments running until her death, leaving an estate of $100,000.

Renovated and long since repurposed, two of Gleim's former brothels—two-story brick commercial buildings—are in the 200 block of West Front Street. Mary Elizabeth Gleeson Gleim (1845–1914) is buried in **Missoula City Cemetery** (2000 Cemetery Rd., grave 2, lot 15, block 71). Tombstones traditionally face east, but before she died Gleim requested that her tombstone face the railroad tracks. That way, she said, she could say goodbye to all the railroad men who had patronized her businesses.

STEVENSVILLE (RAVALLI COUNTY)

The arrival in 1841 of Jesuit missionaries in western Montana's Bitterroot Valley marked the first permanent Euro-American settlement in future Montana. The "blackrobes," as the Salish, or Flathead, tribe called them, had come at the Indians' request to teach them the religion they had heard about from other American Indians who had traveled farther east. Led by Father Pierre-Jean De Smet, the Jesuits built a log mission they named for St. Mary and began converting the Indians to Catholicism. By 1850, discouraged by the Jesuits from hunting buffalo and keeping multiple wives, many of the Salish rebelled. The Jesuits sold the mission for $250 to newly arrived John Owen, who built a wooden stockade around it, added other structures, and began operating it as a trading post known as Fort Owen.

A community called St. Mary's developed around the trading post. In 1864, the settlement's name was changed to Stevensville to honor former territorial governor Isaac Stevens, who had been killed in action during the Civil War. Two years later, the Jesuits sent Father Anthony Ravalli back to Stevensville where he oversaw construction of a church that still stands.

Meanwhile, Owen continued to get along with the tribes in the area, and all was well until his wife Nancy, a Shoshone, died in 1868. Owen began drinking too much and fell into debt, his enterprise ending up on the auction block in 1872.

Little remained of the old mission and trading post when the state acquired a one-acre site around it in 1937. The only standing original structure, called the East Barrack, was built of adobe by the Jesuits. Later archaeological work revealed the foundations of the other buildings, which are visible today. **Fort Owen State Park** (99 Fort Owen Ranch Rd.; 406-273-4253) has interpretive signage. About a mile from the fort site, the 1866 church built by Father Ravalli stands at 315 Charlo Street. It has been restored, and other buildings once part of the mission complex have been reconstructed. A visitor center and museum opened at the site in 1996.

THREE FORKS (GALLATIN COUNTY)

When the Lewis and Clark Expedition finally reached the headwaters of the Missouri River in the summer of 1805, they found three tributaries flowing into it. To be politic, the explorers named the three smaller rivers after the young nation's treasury secretary (Albert Gallatin), the secretary of state (future president James Madison), and the current chief executive (Thomas Jefferson.) They called the point of convergence Three Forks, which later became the name of the town founded in 1908 three miles to the south as a division point on the newly constructed Milwaukee Railroad.

Not that a lot of history didn't happen in the area before then. Long home to American Indians, the Three Forks area later attracted fur traders, mountain men, and eventually settlers. One of those mountain men was John Colter, a civilian member of Lewis and Clark's Corps of Discovery until he decided to leave the party when they passed through in 1806 on their way back down the Missouri. He ended up being the first white man to see what would become Yellowstone National Park and, in 1808, had one of the Old West's more memorable encounters with hostile Indians.

Captured by Blackfeet warriors, he was forced to strip and then told to run for his life. Which is what he did, in the process killing one Indian with his own lance and then diving into the newly named Madison River. Not only did he survive that epic event, but back in the area two years later with a party sent there to build a trading post, he lived through a second Indian fight. This time, he famously wrote in his journal, "I will leave the country day after tomorrow and be damned if I ever come to it again."

The history of the area is the focus of the **Headwaters Heritage Museum** (202 South Main St.; 406-285-4778). Located in an old bank building dating from 1910, the museum has interpretive exhibits and artifacts, including an anvil found at the headwaters. While an anvil may not be the most interesting of artifacts, it is believed to be the oldest known American-made anvil.

VIRGINIA CITY-NEVADA CITY (MADISON COUNTY)

If a lot of gold is coming out of one area, it is logical enough to think there might be more gold to be found in the same region. That's how Virginia City came to be.

A group of Bannack prospectors tried to explore the Yellowstone River, but the resident Crow Indians kept them out. The gold hunters went next to Alder Gulch, about fifty miles from their base in still-booming Bannack. Their logic proved sound—they found ample placer deposits and returned to Bannack for more supplies. All this activity happened in the spring and summer of 1863. A year later, a series of mining camps extended for fourteen miles along the gulch.

The larger of the camps had begun the transition from tent camp to town and needed a name. The desire for wealth was universal, but political inclinations were not. Some of the miners were Southerners who argued for Varina City in honor of Jefferson Davis's wife. The pro-Union men wanted none of that, but when someone proposed Virginia City as a compromise—that commonwealth divided in sentiment over the war—the Southerners agreed. No one seemed to care that the new name might cause confusion given the boomtown status of Virginia City, Nevada.

Virginia City, Montana, quickly overtook Bannack in size and status, gaining the territorial seat of government in less than a year. The capital remained there until 1875 when Helena took over. By that time the gold around Bannack and Virginia City had begun to play out. Even so, it had been quite a ride. In less than a dozen years, the fourteen-mile-long Alder Gulch had given up more than $90 million worth of gold. With improvements in machinery by the turn of the twentieth century, dredging began to pull rich quantities of gold from the gulch, a second-act bonanza that continued into the 1920s. When mining ceased in the area for good, Virginia City lost its economic luster, though it hung on as the county seat.

While Virginia City's early rival, Bannack, has been preserved as a state park, a married couple from Great Falls, Montana, saved the bulk of Virginia City's old buildings. In 1944, Charles and Sue Bovey bought one-hundred-plus buildings in the town and spent the rest of their lives seeing to the town's preservation. They added to the city's inventory of historic structures by moving in old buildings from elsewhere in Montana, including the old railroad depot that became the town's visitor center. In 1961, thanks to their efforts, Virginia City was named a National Historic Landmark.

Nevada City, while it had a different name, was essentially a suburb of Virginia City, only three miles away. It also declined when Virginia City went into a slump following the decline in gold production. But unlike its neighbor, the early twentieth-century dredge mining that gave Virginia City renewed life did not impact Nevada City, which had become a ghost town. The Boveys also acquired buildings in Nevada City and moved other historic structures there from elsewhere.

Virginia City is fourteen miles west of Ennis on State Highway 287. A walking tour giving the history and location of nearly seventy sites is available at the **Virginia City Depot and Visitor Information Center** (413 West Wallace St., Virginia City). The **Nevada City Old Town Museum and Music Hall** (east side of State Highway 287, Nevada City) is a collection of restored vintage buildings with artifacts ranging from gold panning equipment to wagons. The museum also focuses on living history, with reenactors and interactive opportunities for visitors. A train that runs between Nevada City and Virginia City can be boarded at the Bovey Center, across the highway from the museum.

INDEX

ABOUT THE AUTHOR

An elected member of the Texas Institute of Letters, **Mike Cox** is the author of more than thirty-five nonfiction books. Over an award-winning freelance career dating back to his high school days, he has written hundreds of newspaper articles and columns, magazine stories, and essays for a wide variety of regional and national publications. When not writing, he spends as much time as he can traveling, fishing, hunting, and looking for new stories to tell. He lives in the Hill Country village of Wimberley, Texas.

To learn more about the author and his work, visit www.mike coxauthor.com.